Under The Pine Boughs

Under The
Pine Boughs

(Short Stories
of
Homespun Living)

Mary Alice Carlson

XULON PRESS

Xulon Press
2301 Lucien Way #415
Maitland, FL 32751
407.339.4217
www.xulonpress.com

© 2019 by Mary Alice Carlson

All rights reserved solely by the author. The author guarantees all contents are original and do not infringe upon the legal rights of any other person or work. No part of this book may be reproduced in any form without the permission of the author. The views expressed in this book are not necessarily those of the publisher.

Scripture quotations taken from the King James Version (KJV) –*public domain*.

Printed in the United States of America.

ISBN-13: 9781545675243

Dedication

This compilation of short stories is dedicated to family and friends who have inspired and enriched my life.

Table of Contents

Dedication v
Active Faith ix
Authors Note xiii

Under the Pine Boughs
(Short stories of homespun living)

The Matriarch 3
Independence Day 7
Spring on the Farm 10
The Beach Party 15
A Dear Friend in an Unexpected Place 19
The Journey to Historic Route 66 23
Sensible Shoes 27
Facing the Sun 31
Hope 35
Take the Long Way Home 38
Big Oak 42
Coming Home 46

The Traveler 50
Traveler's Gift 54
A Winter Guardian Angel 58
Leaving the Nest 62
Beaver Battle.......................... 66
Save the Last Dance for Me 69
A Leap of Faith 74
The Christmas Tree 77
Laddie and the Lost Shoe 81
Till the Cows Come Home 85
The Sugar Incident 89
Moose Lake State Hospital 92
The Little Yellow Dress................. 97
Murphy's Law........................101
Beaunitta............................. 105
Remembering Evelyne 108
Christmas 112
Canning.............................. 116
Veteran's Day Thanksgiving 120
Dot's First Christmas 123
Straw Hat 126
Remembering Emma 129
My Christmas Story 133
The Big Storm....................... 137
The Quilt............................141
Walking the Rim 145

Forward

Active Faith
by Burton Laine

I can't think of a better way to describe Mary Alice Carlson than active faith. I've known her since she was a teenager traveling with her father, Pastor Phill, with a rollicking performing group that inspired generations of people at churches throughout the region. It gave her a faith base to work from that has served her well.

As editor of The Senior Reporter magazine, I've never limited her stories to a word count. I just trust that every word she writes is important, and at the end she will inspire. I don't have to say how inspirational her stories are to our readers. They tell me. Over the years,

I've had more positive comments on her stories than any other writer in our magazine. The most common thing I hear is: "I love Mary Alice's stories. It's the first thing I read when I receive the magazine."

There are several writers in the magazine, and I have to admit, when all the stories are turned in for each issue, hers is the first one I read also. I am glad to see she has compiled some of her best into this volume.

Mary Alice lives her faith in her life. As a college professor, she sees her students as individuals and wants to inspire them to look at their lives with promise.

In her local church, she has taken on leadership roles but still sits on the floor with children at church services to tell them stories. I know she puts as much time into preparing for these children as she does with everything else in her life. She does this as her 95-year-old father sits with the congregation and watches with pride.

Mary Alice is a multiple award-winning writer. She has won Awards of Excellence for her personal essays though the North American Mature Publishers Association. These awards have meaning because the stories are weighed against writers from across the country and have to meet high standards that they could appear in any of the publications and be appreciated.

Through these stories, you spend time with Mary Alice on her rural farm in northern Minnesota. You are invited into her home. You travel with her. And she shares some of her most intimate life experiences. Her descriptions are rich, and you will feel everything she feels in every story.

Whether you grew up in a rural farming community or yearned to have the experience, you will enjoy these real-life emotional stories from Mary Alice.

Authors Note

For ten years I have had the tremendous opportunity of writing a column for the *Senior Reporter* magazine based out of Duluth Minnesota. This book is a collection of several of the columns that have been published in the magazine. There is a story within every story contained in this compilation. If you listen carefully you may find moments of your own life reflected in the pages of this book.

These stories are all true life experiences. Some of them are filled with joy, others with laughter, and some with tears. But all of the stories express my desire to live life with a heart filled with gratefulness to God in all circumstances.

Rejoice always, pray without ceasing, in everything give thanks, for this is the will of God in Christ Jesus for you. Thessalonians 5:16-18. (KJV)

Under the Pine Boughs

(Short stories of homespun living)

The Matriarch
by Mary Alice Carlson

Forty-one years ago as newlyweds, my husband and I walked the acreage of a tumble-down, falling-over old farmstead in Carlton County. With big dreams of owning a place of our own, we ignored obvious problems with the house and barn. A beaver pond and swamp sat right in the middle of the 80 acres, but the surrounding woods were beautiful. Almost by accident, we found what would become our greatest treasure.

On the back side of the beaver pond more than a quarter of a mile away from the house, she stands. She is a stunning white pine. Somehow she was missed when this area was logged many years ago, and I think she was saved by the beaver pond when the Moose Lake fire roared through here in the early 1900s. When we first bushwhacked our way to her through all of the undergrowth, we couldn't believe the size of her trunk. And we couldn't touch our fingers when we held hands and tried to reach around her. We guesstimated she was about 12 feet around. Her first branch was 30 feet up, and when the wind blew through her branches, it sounded like singing.

Needless to say, we bought the old farm. We were full of vigor and believed we could make some dreams come true here. But, for some reason, we were both very reverent about the tree. The first 10 years we lived here, she watched the house and barns be restored. She met our children one by one. She saw the cattle and chickens and heard the laughter of children. She withstood terrible storms and awful winters. And yet, she thrived.

During the next 10 years, she lost her biggest branch during a lightning strike. Two years later, her top was hit again by lightning and she lost that. Never daunted by seemingly fatal blows, she continued to grow. A new leader branch appeared two years later, and the top of the tree began to take form again.

The Matriarch

We have celebrated Christmas for years in the place where she casts her early morning shadow. We hiked out to see her again in December to measure her at her base. She's a boastful 16 feet around.

That measurement might be close to 200 years old. I can only imagine what she has seen and heard, and can bear witness to. My hope is that she will double her age, weather the storms, and continue to flourish and grow. Our kitchen window on the east side of the house frames her perfectly. She is in the sunrise. She is the first thing I see in the morning and the last thing at twilight. I have lived 41 years in her glorious shadow.

During every season of the year, we've hiked back to see her and sit in her shadow. She stands tall like a sentinel and guardian overseeing the farm. Her presence makes me feel safe and secure at this place we call home.

Somehow over the past 41 years, I've become tied to her. Although my life expectancy is much shorter than hers, my roots run deep on this old farm and so do hers. She and I have both endured terrible storms. There have even been a few times in my life when life events have made me feel like I've been struck by lightning. But each time I've recovered slowly like her and continued to grow. My age is showing in the lines on my face and hers in the grooves of her bark.

She has seen it all and still raises her branches in praise to the Creator for every moment of trial or joy. She is the matriarch of the farm, and peace drips from her branches. And the song that flows through her needles is the greatest treasure of all.

Independence Day

For years our little family has participated in the Fourth of July celebrations in our rural area. Moose Lake has a wonderful parade and a host of other activities to access. For years our girls were a part of the parade, and we would sit on the curb and wave to them as they walked by on the parade route. The best part of the whole parade was when the 148th Fighter jets flew over the parade route. The crowd would stand and wave and cheer them as they barreled through the sky.

When our first Fourth of July arrived as "empty nesters," my husband announced early in the morning that he really wasn't interested in attending the parade. He wanted to just stay home and get some work done outside. I was agreeable but told him I was really going to miss seeing the jets fly over.

At about 10 o'clock that morning, he came running up to the house, yelling at me to grab the life jackets and jump in the truck. When I got outside, the canoe was loaded, and he was revving the engine. I jumped in and asked him what was going on. All he would say was that we had to hurry and I would have the best Fourth of July ever. I must have looked terrified as we peeled out of the driveway.

Within a few minutes, we arrived at a local lake, and my husband untied the canoe and ran carrying it to the lake. He kept yelling at me to hurry. So I grabbed the life jackets and paddles and ran down to the shore. Within moments, we were on the water, and he kept saying, "paddle faster." Finally, I asked what we were doing. He wanted us to get to the middle of the lake as fast as we could. As we were gliding across the water, he stopped us and said, "They're coming! Can you hear them?" I closed my eyes and listened carefully.

First it came as a rumble, and then it got so loud that I could feel it in my chest, and then just over the treetops came the 148th Fighter jets. I was so excited I almost jumped out of the canoe. I lifted my canoe paddle and waved it and cheered. In a moment, they had crossed the lake and were banking southward. I continued to wave my paddle, and then something happened that took my breath away. They had banked south but did a quick turn and came right over the top of us. I waved my canoe paddle and sobbed as they disappeared into the southern sky. Both of us sat quietly in the canoe listening to the fading sound of the jets as they made their way to the local parades.

We were both so moved by the event that neither of us could speak. It took some time to hear the lapping of the water on the side of the canoe. We were so filled with awe. Those pilots gave us a great gift on that Fourth of July. It is a gift that brings tears to my eyes when I consider the sacrifice and protection they represent. It's the gift of freedom.

Spring on the Farm

Spring is finally here! I so enjoy the warm sunshine and the relief from the seeping cold of winter. Spring around the farm always brings an enormous amount of work. But we work happily at the repairs and the cleanup after a long winter. Spring also arrives with new responsibilities. There will be newly hatched chicks in the brooder and the anticipation of the birth of the calves. I love when the babies are born, and I am hesitant to leave the farm when the time of delivery is near.

I have recorded breeding dates and due dates for years. I know what to look for and how to tell when a cow is close to delivery. I have incubated eggs and watched in wonder on the 21st day as the eggs hatch. I can spot distress in an animal, and I know when to call the vet. I actually

Spring On The Farm

was proud of myself for being so intuitive with the animals. As it turns out, I'm not nearly as brilliant as I thought I was. So let me tell you why.

My husband and I had been invited to take our horses to St. Croix State Park over Memorial Day weekend in May. Some friends of ours had invited us to join them and ride the horse trails and camp. We were so excited, we could hardly wait to get there. We would be within an hour of home should anything go wrong at the farm. We planned to be gone for three days. This was a perfect setup. The cows weren't due to calf for another week. So we jumped at the chance, and I asked my father to do chores while we were gone. He was more than happy to help out, so we did chores, carefully checked on every animal on the place, loaded up the horses and the dog, and drove away at 6 p.m. on Friday.

I called my dad the next morning at 8 a.m. He had been to the farm and done chores at 6 a.m. When I asked him how things at the farm were, there was a long pause. Then he carefully explained to me that apparently I had a due date wrong because Dolly had calved during the night and there was a beautiful Herford calf lying in the manure in the corral when he got to the farm. He had moved the cow and calf into a loafing shed and closed the door so that the cow and calf were bedded in straw and away from the rest of the herd. He said all was well and we shouldn't come home. We should enjoy our time away and ride as much as we could. I felt a little guilty but knew things were fine at home, so we saddled up and rode all day.

I called on Sunday morning at 8 a.m. Dad wasn't back from the farm yet, so I called an hour later. Again I asked Dad how chores went, and I thought he wasn't going to answer the question. He told me I had another due date wrong. Apparently, Hannah had calved in the early morning, and there was an Angus calf lying in the manure in the corral. He attempted to get her into the loafing shed. But when he opened the shed door to get Hannah in, Dolly and her new calf ran out the door. He assured me that everything was fine, and he didn't want me to worry. He said I should just ride my horse and have a good time. How on earth could I have been so wrong on the calving dates? I spoke with my husband about it and we decided we would try to stay one more night and enjoy the campfire and food, get a good night's sleep, and call Dad the next morning.

I called Dad on Monday morning at 8 a.m. There was no answer. I called again at 9 a.m., still no answer. I called at 10 a.m. after we had packed up most of our camping gear. Breathlessly, he answered the phone. I asked him if everything was all right. He told me to "get home," as there were calves everywhere and he was a nervous wreck. We loaded up the horses and headed home.

When we arrived at the farm, both Mom and Dad were standing leaning on the corral gate looking at the beautiful calves and their moms. The cows were contentedly eating hay, and the calves were lying in dry spots sleeping in the sunshine. Dad asked me if I enjoyed my time away. He knew I had needed a break from the work at home. I told him I had a wonderful time and was so grateful to him for caring for the animals while we were gone. He put his arm around me and told me he would be glad to help me anytime except for during calving season. He hadn't slept much during the past three nights. Then he gave me a kiss on the forehead and said, "Aren't those the most beautiful calves in the world?" My Dad had become a farmer in three short days. And I decided I wasn't as smart as I thought I was.

The Beach Party

January and February can be daunting months of cold, darkness and heavy snow here in northern Minnesota. One year it became so oppressive I thought we would never be released from winter's icy grip. I remember it well, wearing almost every piece of cold weather gear I owned, shoveling my way to the barn, feeding the animals, shoveling a path to the manure pile, cleaning the barn, and shoveling my way back to the house. My hands were so chapped I slept with gloves on to protect them. We all struggled to remain optimistic about the coming of spring.

Just when I thought we would get relief, an arctic blast came out of Canada that was predicted to last a week. I had finally had enough. I called up the family and announced that

Under The Pine Boughs

during this terrible cold snap, I was throwing a beach party at our home. But there were rules for attending this event. You needed to wear your best Hawaiian shirt, wear your favorite shorts, bring a lawn chair, and wear your sunglasses. Party start time was 1:00, and by the way, don't be late.

Two days before the party I started moving furniture out of the living room, and my husband gave me that look I so appreciate—the one that silently says "this is crazy." But he helped with all the heavy furniture and soon we had an empty living room with a few lawn chairs facing the large post between the living room, dining room and entry. I had a stack of brown paper bags that I was making huge palm leaves out of, and he pitched right in and taped them to the top of the post and the ceiling. Then we blew up balloons and decorated them to look like coconuts. We were going for the Hawaiian look on a shoe string budget. I decided the menu would be a summertime favorite of sloppy Joes and potato salad, fresh vegetables and lemonade.

When the extended family arrived, we jumped into a few cars and drove to the bowling alley. I'm sure the personnel at the bowling alley

The Beach Party

thought we were nuts. It was so cold that day that some of my family members didn't wear shorts. But everyone had on Hawaiian shirts and sunglasses. Keeping with the spirit of the party, my mom wore jeans and wool socks with sandals. We had a tremendous time bowling and then came back to the house to listen to the Beach Boys sing about summertime and have our picnic lunch in our lawn chairs under the giant palm tree in the living room. My husband cranked up the wood stove so that the inside temperature was close to 80 degrees. Laughter filled the house, and suddenly it wasn't so cold and dark any more. We all carried on as though it was the most beautiful summer day we had ever experienced. We even had ice cream for desert.

It was chore time when the party broke up, and as I headed to the barn I didn't seem to notice the biting wind. I was lost in thought about the fun afternoon, and I found myself chuckling as I fed the animals. We put all of the furniture back in the living room that evening but left the palm tree where she stood. It was a great reminder that winter wouldn't last forever.

About a week later, I had a visit with one of my extended family members. She thanked

Under The Pine Boughs

me for the beach party and told me the party had been an attitude adjuster. It had lifted the darkness of winter for her. I told her I had had the same experience, and I was so happy she had attended.

Now every February when I start fussing about the cold and snow, and when the blast of artic air creeps over us from Canada, I make potato salad and sloppy Joes. I put on my wool socks and sandals, and while I'm eating I remind myself that this current condition is only temporary. Spring is on her way.

A Dear Friend in an Unexpected Place

I have discovered precious people in a variety of venues. Mostly it's my day-to-day encounters that nurture precious friendships, but I have a long-standing relationship with a precious woman who is really my hero. We don't see each other every week. Our encounters happen about every eight weeks, and we've spent 41 years building our relationship. She has a very special talent, and nobody on this earth can do what she does for me. She takes care of my unruly hair at her salon.

My mom discovered her when she was fresh out of cosmetology school and instantly built a friendship that would span decades. In the 1970s when I had long hair that I could sit on, she gave me a haircut that would withstand the tropical climate of South America. My long hair was gone, but in her wisdom she gave me just what I needed. And I'm not sure I ever thanked her for that first haircut. It was perfect.

Following my return, I began to frequent her shop about every eight weeks. Over the course of a few years, she started a family. I got engaged, and she did everyone's hair for my wedding. She even slipped in to the wedding and left a beautiful gift. When I got pregnant, she gave me a short manageable haircut that really was wonderfully easy when our first daughter arrived. She, too, had a second child, and as our families grew, we shared pictures and stories of our children. We talked about life and about family, and we prayed for each other.

Subsequently, my girls and husband became regulars at her shop. With love and kindness, she managed to have us look our best for prom, job interviews, graduations, family reunions and every other big event in our lives. My mom had her hair done every Saturday for 40 years, and she looked like a million bucks when she walked out of the shop. Who knew what an impact Barb would have on our lives.

Barb supported us through the ups and downs; she cheered when we had happy times and she cried with us when things were tough. When my mom passed away, it was Barb who went to the funeral home and did my mom's hair one last time. It was Barb who called me to check on me 10 weeks after the funeral because I had not called to make an appointment. It was Barb who lovingly hugged me when I got to the shop and allowed me to share my grief with her. It was Barb who wrangled my unruly hair and eased my anxiety. What a precious friend.

Both of us have experienced great sorrow and great happiness in our lives. For more than 41 years, we've fostered a rock solid relationship of trust in each other and faith in God. We don't meet for coffee or talk on the phone, but I know deep down in my heart that when I need her she will be there, and I believe she knows the same about me. I have been blessed, encouraged, supported and loved by a wonderful woman whose skills are far greater than those she uses as a hair stylist. It's about time I step up and thank her.

Barb, I'm grateful for all you have done for our family. Your impact on our family is eternal.

God has blessed me in so many ways through you over the years. And, Barb, you know that cape you put around my neck when I'm in the shop? You should be wearing it because in my eyes you are a super hero with a heart of gold.

The Journey to Historic Route 66

While on vacation, my husband and I had the wonderful opportunity to catch a ride into the Black Mountains of Arizona. We were in search of a nearly abandoned town on old Route 66. The town's name is Oatman. As we drove into the mountains, Nat King Cole's song kept playing in my mind. The famous line, "Get your kicks on Route 66," had me smiling and bouncing along in the compact car. I was surprised when we rounded the final corner and took in the view.

The first buildings were abandoned and falling in on themselves. I actually felt my anxiety rise to escape level when we parked in a "blow your tires out" rocky, scary, open area behind a crumbling shed. I had a feeling there were no kicks to be had on Route 66 this day for me. Boy, was I wrong!

We climbed up from the rock quarry into the east end of town and there were wild burros everywhere. Being an animal lover, I figured I should at least walk Route 66 through this old town. Crumbling buildings, rustic old shops, an old hotel and two ancient restaurants greeted me. The burros were up on the wooden walkways in front of the stores and shops. Travelers like me were feeding them hay cubes. The old west town was hot, dirty and dusty. For some unknown reason, I felt right at home.

We had a delightful lunch in one of the restaurants. Not everyone would choose to eat there. It was really rustic, but the burgers were awesome. We strolled through the town ducking in and out of shops wondering why Oatman had almost become a ghost town. It seems the old Route 66 was too dangerous for travelers, so in the 1950s a new road was built through the mountains miles from Oatman, and the town died. But in the 1940s, it was a hot spot between Chicago and California. Movie stars stayed here, and mining was booming in the Black Mountains.

The Journey To Historic Route 66

While I was walking on old Route 66, I had a nagging memory about my mom. I remembered hearing a story she shared with me when I was a little girl. In 1942, at the age of 16, she decided to strike out on her own and bought a one-way ticket on the bus heading for California. Mom loved the song *Get your Kicks on Route 66* because that was the road she traveled from Chicago to California. I quickly called my 92-year-old dad to confirm the story. He told me it was all true and after three months in sunny California working for the phone company, Mom bought a ticket home to Chicago and traveled Route 66 once again.

So there I was crying my eyes out standing on Route 66 imagining my mom filled with anticipation when the bus stopped in the town of Oatman. She was just a kid then on a huge adventure, excited about every turn in the road. And there I was visualizing Mom's blue eyes sparkling and her beautiful brown hair blowing around her face. When they said it was time to go, I didn't want to leave. I went into a shop and bought a T-shirt in mom's favorite color that reads, "Oatman Arizona, the Mother Road, Route 66." Those words were the truest for me.

What do I remember most about my vacation? Oatman! It's where I crossed paths with my mom 75 years apart and felt closer to her than I had since she died three years ago. And it's where my own adventuring spirit was boosted.

Sensible Shoes

I met Sensible Shoes in the late 1970s when she was well into her 60s, and I was in my early 20s. She was short and strong and stubborn, and wasn't afraid to correct you if she thought your behavior, language or ideas just weren't to her standard. Sensible Shoes had been widowed for more than 30 years; she had raised five children, lived alone in a small house in town, and was the kindest person I've ever had the privilege to know.

When I first met her, I was dating her grandson. She looked me up and down, turned on her heel, and sat down across the room. I remember thinking I was doomed, and she hadn't even spoken with me. The next time I met her was at my wedding shower. She made it very clear to me that I was not family yet. I was very concerned that I would never meet her approval. Most people would probably just ignore her, but for some reason I thought it was important that I break through that tough exterior and find out what was really on the inside.

I learned two very important things about Sensible Shoes in my first few months of marriage. She was a real "bulldog" when it came to playing cards. She liked to win. And she made the world's best rye bread every Saturday. Add to this the fact that late at night she would sew quilts for all of her grandchildren and great-grandchildren. She braided rugs and crocheted table runners. She attended church several times a week and had a deep faith that kept her moving forward in life despite the loss of two children and the death of her husband.

Before our first anniversary, my husband and I went to visit her on her own turf. We went alone to her house on a Saturday, and the smell of fresh rye bread filled the entire kitchen. We ate bread together, as she and my husband talked about his childhood and all of the things she let him get away with. Laughter filled the tiny kitchen, and then she quizzed me about my life and my faith, and when we got ready to leave, she hugged me.

Sensible Shoes wasn't as scary as I had been led to believe. We wrote letters back and forth, and we shared our concerns with one another. I prayed for her and she prayed for me. But she still made me nervous. On our first anniversary, we invited her to come with the rest of my husband's family to our little tumbled down farm. I was worried that the food wouldn't be up to standard and that the old house wouldn't be clean enough. Frankly, I was just plain worried that this event was going to be a disaster.

Imagine my surprise when she got to the farm with five loaves of the best rye bread in the world. Sensible Shoes was happy to be at our farm. She talked with me about having grown up on a farm, having married a farmer, and how much she loved farm life. Our bantam hen with 10 chicks was loose in the yard, and Sensible Shoes laughed and laughed at the antics of the chicks. Her favorite animals were the workhorses, and as she looked out at our lone horse standing in the pasture, years of her life seemed to drop away, and I saw how beautiful she really was on the inside and outside.

She enjoyed the day, the food and the company. Before her ride left the driveway, she hugged me once again and I knew at that moment I was family. I had the great privilege of knowing her for the next 20 years. Sensible Shoes went home to heaven to gather with her family around the throne of God when she was in her 90s. We buried her next to her husband and children in a small cemetery behind a Lutheran church in southern Minnesota.

So as Mother's Day is approaching, I want to wish Grandma Ada a Happy Grandmother's Day and thank her for being Sensible Shoes in my life. Her beautiful quilts are still on the beds, and her indelible mark is still on my heart.

Facing the Sun

⧞

In April of 2016, I was searching for a creative idea to share with the children in our parish. While shopping at the local feed store, I came across a display of sunflower seeds and curiously explored the many different varieties. I always have been fascinated by sunflowers, but in my 60 years I have never grown any. The research bug bit me, and when I got home I delved into all of the available information I could get ahold of on the computer.

I had always wondered why when I drove west across North Dakota in the morning, the sunflower heads were facing me and when I drove east in the evening, the sunflower heads were still facing me. As it turns out, sunflowers are "phototrophic." That means they reach for the sun at daybreak and follow it across the sky all day long and then face west as the sun goes down. They rest during the night and then turn and face east again in the morning. The sunlight they reach for is the biggest encourager of their growth. How amazing is that? I got so excited about the sunflower's behavior I knew I had to share the story. Thus began my five-month journey with sunflowers.

I would like to say I bought a few packets of seeds to share with the children, but the truth is I bought a lot of packets. I was having trouble containing myself because I do believe we spend too much time looking down in our lives and not enough time looking up. Children and adults have issues that cause them to lower their eyes and be downcast in spirit when all they see are problems and shadows. If we want to optimize our growth potential, I think we should take a lesson from the sunflowers and start looking up.

The children were thrilled with the message, and I brought home several packets of the seeds that were left over after I distributed them. My youngest grandson Jonas and I planted them in little pots and placed them in the east window of our living room. Within a week, they were up and leaning toward the window. I sent six pots home for Jonas to plant at his house, and I planted the rest in the flower garden alongside the driveway.

As they started to take root, I had the opportunity to watch them every day as they grew. East to west, they leaned as they grew by the inch and then suddenly by the foot. Some grew to four feet tall—others to six, eight and ten feet. When their faces opened, they were so beautiful that every day when I walked out to get the mail, I stood at the garden in absolute wonder at their growth and beauty. And every day I got to watch the sunflowers follow the sun.

In August we had a terrible storm with high winds and heavy rain. Trees all over northern Minnesota had toppled in the winds. Power was out everywhere, and our road had washed out. The next morning I went out to look at the sunflowers. Half of them had been blown over and were lying on the ground. I was sick to my stomach about it but knew there was nothing I could do. Within a week, the downed sunflowers had turned their faces back to the sun. Even though they were badly bent and terribly injured, they still reached to the sun for optimal growth even after a disaster. By September they still had the bends and curves from the storm but they were almost upright once again. This was a tremendous lesson for me.

I've had times in my life when I have felt terribly bent and injured emotionally, spiritually and physically. Sometimes it has been about a relationship, finances or health issues. And I'll admit that I have spent too much time looking down at problems and issues, and not enough time looking up. To become who the Creator made me to be, I need to keep looking up. I want to fill my life with light for optimal growth.

The flower heads have gone to seed now, and the birds have enjoyed a harvest of nutrition. I have gathered some of the seeds and will plant them again next spring. Inside of each seed is the desire to reach for the sunlight. What an example. My greatest hope is that I will never forget this experience or treat it as mundane. For as long as I have breath I, too, want reach for the sunshine.

Hope

The cold days of winter will soon be over, and I wait patiently for the warm winds of springtime to awaken the earth from its winter nap. As the daylight hours extend, I find myself filled with anticipation of what is to come. Nestled in the early springtime, this year is the celebration of Easter. For many, Easter is a celebration of baskets and candies and springtime. In our home, it is a celebration of renewed faith and hope.

Three years ago at Easter time, I found myself floundering in despair, hoping the holiday would soon be over so that I could get moving on the many projects slated to be finished. At that time, I was also involved at our local parish leading the Sunday services and filling in the gaps while we looked for a new pastor. I was tired and disgruntled and ill. I just didn't think I could handle one more obligation effectively. But I was committed to finishing up my assigned tasks and taking a good rest when I was done.

At our parish, Easter Sunday begins with the traditional "Blooming of the Cross". A large wooden cross stands in the front of the church that is wrapped in chicken wire. As the people arrive for the service, they are given beautiful flowers–carnations, roses, daisies, mums–that are all different colors. At the start of the service, hymns of great joy fill the church, and the parishioners come forward and thread the blossoms into the wire on the cross. It is very moving to watch and participate in this act of faith and hope, and the resulting cross covered with flowers is breath–taking. But on this particular year, I just wanted it to be over.

Then it happened. We had extra flowers in the back of the church, so I called all of the children forward to insert the remaining flowers onto the cross. I had dropped to my knees at the cross to hand the children the blossoms, and she came up the aisle to take the flowers from my hands. She was about four years old, dressed in a beautiful

Hope

pale pink dress. She had long blond hair tied back with a beautiful ribbon that matched her dress. Her eyes were light blue and her smile was enchanting. As I knelt at the foot of the cross with her it occurred to me that all of the other children had returned to their seats. When she placed the last flower in on the cross, right where we would have expected the feet of Jesus to have been, she looked deep into my eyes, smiled, and said, "Happy Easter." I burst into tears as she headed back down the aisle to her family.

I looked for her after the service. I was unable to find her. I inquired about who she was and what her family name was. No one knew. Everyone saw her as we placed the flowers on the cross but no one could identify her. While driving home from church, I decided her name must be Hope. For that is exactly what she filled my heart with on that Easter morning. I carry her memory tucked safely in my heart, and I thank my Heavenly Father for meeting my needs at the foot of the cross on Easter morning.

May the celebration of Easter fill your heart with hope for the days ahead.

Take the Long Way Home

My dad enjoys a manicured lawn, beautiful landscaping and bright flowers strategically planted to set off the house and yard. As long as I can remember, he has been the chief lawn mower and bush trimmer. With great care he trims, mows, waters and fertilizes. For many years, I have accompanied him to several garden centers looking for just the right flowers to plant in his four oak half-barrels and in the four flower beds that flank the house and backyard. This year was no exception.

Dad had asked me to go with him in early May. My schedule was packed and it wasn't till later in the month that he caught me at home and reminded me of my commitment. He explained that he had already been to several places north of Barnum and found nothing to his liking. So together we headed south. On a whim we went to the small town of Askov looking for a Garden Center that had been advertised in the local paper. We had to stop and ask directions, but we were overjoyed with the selection of plants. I helped pick out the plants he wanted, and with smiles on our faces and all of the plants securely placed in his car we, headed for home.

Instead of turning around and going back the way we came, Dad headed north on a road neither of us had ever been on before. The drive was exceptionally beautiful for me. We were in farm country. Around the first corner was a pond with a pair of geese and their babies out for a swim. Several fields close to the road had cows with their calves resting in the sun. Farther up the winding road was a field filled with ewes and their lambs. I especially liked the little black lamb standing in a field of white heads. Lilacs were in bloom and nestled around farm houses. The grass was so green and lush I almost wanted to leap from the car and take a stroll in the fields. Then I had a revelation…

Every time I drive somewhere, everyone is in a hurry. People are impatient and rude on the road. But years ago we used to go for a Sunday drive. My dad would drive me to a hidden valley to look at the horses out in the field. We would take our time and pull off the road so I could get a good look at the animals. In the fall we went where the maple trees were filling the sky with colors of orange, yellow and red. We even took these drives in the winter to look at Christmas lights. I did this with my own children and somehow I had forgotten the wonder of it all.

Dad and I got lost on our way back from Askov. Thanks to a Fed-Ex driver (who had a map) we found our way back to the main road. But I didn't want the ride to end. It seemed too short. Our last stop was the Dairy Queen, just like it was years ago in another place and time. I felt refreshed when I got home, and I wondered why we hadn't taken the time to go for a Sunday drive in so many years. When my husband got home from work I told him about my experience. He doesn't think he's ever been down that road either. He wants to go and look, and see, and enjoy the wonder of a Sunday drive once again.

I'm going to be thinking about the drive with my dad for an extended period of time. I need to step away from the hustle and hurry that can be so consuming. Thanks dad for the Sunday drive on a Friday afternoon. And, dad, it's really wonderful to me if we "take the long way home."

Big Oak

In August, I went to see my brother and his wife who live in Apple Valley, Minnesota. I drove down early on a Wednesday morning so that my brother and I could have the day to visit. We did a little shopping and had a bite to eat together, and then he said he wanted to go back to our childhood neighborhood to reminisce and see what was still left after 50 years. I was a little hesitant but agreed that neither of us would ever return there without the other. So off we went to explore what remained of our childhood neighborhood.

As we drove through the old neighborhood, it became very clear that because we were constantly together as children, he carried half of each memory and I carried the other half. I remembered most of the names of our

Big Oak

neighbors, and he remembered every neighbor's dog's name. We talked about many of our adventures and the names of all the children we played with, rode bikes with, built forts with, and most of all…climbed Big Oak with.

Big Oak has always been and will always be the center of our childhood memories. The oak tree was massive and had a rope swing hanging from one of the upper branches. Every giant branch had a name and if you could climb to the king's chair, you were at the very top of the tree. We spent hours daily under the tree and shaded from the sun up in the branches. The tree was located in a valley behind one of the neighbor's homes, and it was not unusual for 12 to 15 of the neighborhood children to be up in the tree or swinging on the rope swing at the same time.

Amazingly, when we drove to the home behind which Big Oak stood, the same name was on the mailbox as was 50 years ago. My brother pulled into the driveway and suggested we knock on the door. After a minute or two, the front door opened and standing there was my second mom. She is 92, and I haven't seen her for over 20 years. She knew who we were instantly and invited us into the house. I was moved to tears as we visited. I was so happy to have had the opportunity to see her again and to thank her for granting us the privilege of happy memories growing up in the shade of the Big Oak tree. Then she said, "Big Oak still stands in the valley, and you are welcome to go and see her."

As we walked down the hill and into the valley, everything was just as I remembered. The flood of memories was overwhelming. Big Oak has kept time with me and 50 years later she is just as majestic and huge as she was when I was eight years old. I still can't reach the first branch, and her gnarled bark bears witness to the children who played day after day up in the tree. I cried as I put my hands on the tree. I felt as though I had returned "home" once more with my brother by my side. He snapped a picture of me standing next to the base of the tree and then said something funny because he knew I would soon be reduced to a puddle of tears. As we walked up the hill, we both turned and looked one more time at Big Oak. In my heart, the childhood memory and the new memory were a perfect match.

I never said goodbye to Big Oak when we were leaving because she knows I'll be back.

I'll return over and over again when I reminisce about the best years of my childhood. There is enormous peace and happiness in her presence and laughter in her branches. They say you can never return home again, but they are wrong. I walked down the hill and into the valley, and she was still waiting for me.

Coming Home

I rejoiced with exceeding joy the arrival of warm days and green grass. I was so happy when the snow bank on the north side of the barn melted that I did a little dance in the yard holding the rake. We have a low spot in the yard that retains a lot of water in the spring, and I have watched with great joy my geese swim and bathe themselves in the short-term pond that the rain and melting snow have created. But this year, I got the surprise of my life while watching the geese from the living room window.

Four years ago, upon the death of my goose "Nathan," my husband drove countless miles to a hatchery and came home with two goslings and two mallard ducklings. I raised them on the back porch, making sure to hold them daily and nurture them to the best of my ability. We enjoyed

Coming Home

countless hours watching the ducks take wing and practice their flying skills first by circling our farm and then expanding their flights down the driveway and circling our neighbor's home. They would spend the morning practicing their flight patterns, return to the coop for food and a nap, and then resume flying in the evenings. The drake mallard left in the fall when a flock of mallards called to him from the sky.

The female mallard stayed the winter of her first year and then took wing in early June close to her first birthday. She did return the following spring with a handsome drake and spent a few days in the short-term pond in the front yard. How did I know it was her? When I came out of the house to feed the chickens, she strutted out of the pond and followed me to the coop door, quacking her usual greeting. I was pleased to see her and happy to throw some corn out for her to enjoy as a snack.

I have celebrated her happy life for the past four years and wondered where she spends her winters. I'm sure she has been to places in the United States that I have never seen. Last year, I was sure that her journey had come to an end either during hunting season or by some other means. It was time for me to store her in my memory and stop looking for her in April. It was time for me to let her go.

In early May of this year, the temporary pond in the front yard was still full of snow and ice. Gradually, it filled with water, and I turned out the geese for a day of fun in the sun. The next morning we let the geese out of the coop and while wrapped in a heavy robe drinking coffee with my husband, something large flew by the living room window. He jumped up and looked outside exclaiming, "She's home!" I was an unbeliever and slow to respond. But, sure enough, there she was in the yard headed toward the chicken coop, quacking all the way. In the early mornings when I would go out to do chores, I could hear her quacking as she circled the house in the air. She stayed for two weeks with her handsome drake and then disappeared when the temporary pond dried up. I believe she is nesting close by in one of the many wetland areas around our farm.

"Home" is a beacon for her. No matter how far she travels, or the vast amount of peril she has faced, she remembers how to return. I'm so happy I still live on the farm and can be a witness to her story. My life story is very similar to hers. I have been blessed with so many incredible experiences during my lifetime that have served to draw me closer to the Creator. I, too, am imprinted with a beacon. But my beacon is a spiritual one that, as the years pass, is signaling me to a heavenly home. During this life I, too, have faced much peril. But in the end when I arrive, the shout will go up ... she's home!

The Traveler

The Traveler arrived here on the farm sometime close to December eighth. I caught a glimpse of beautiful hazel eyes when I was out in the barn doing chores. During the next few days the temperature plummeted well below zero, and with the deep snow I decided food must be provided. My husband cautioned me about feeding one who would surely be moving on, but I was so concerned for the Traveler that I took a bowl of food to the barn. I placed the food in a stall where hay is stacked to the ceiling but at the doorway is only waist high.

Several days passed and several bowls of food were consumed. On Friday, December 13, I went to the barn well after the sun had set and while I was throwing hay, I spotted the Traveler. Very cautiously and quietly I filled the bowl and

The Traveler

shut the stall door. I watched the shadow of the Traveler come down from the stacked hay and warily approach the bowl of food. I cooed in a low voice, and hazel eyes were lifted to my face. I removed my glove and reached my arm through the stall boards in her direction. Carefully, approaching my outstretched fingers the Traveler pushed the crown of her head against my fingers and started to purr.

It took several more days before we had a relationship where she was unafraid to peek out at me from atop the hay bales. Then one night in the dark while doing chores without a flashlight, I fumbled with the stall door and like an unseeing person searched for the food bowl. While I was bent over pouring food into the bowl, the Traveler rubbed my face with her nose. I was spellbound. In the darkness, she had approached and was unafraid. I cautiously petted her.

Determined to make friends, I began spending more time in the daylight sitting on the bales of hay in the stall. Five days before Christmas she approached me. I now understand her wariness. Traveler's front leg is shattered. It's an old injury that is healed, but she cannot navigate the deep snow. Her front leg is warm but dangles loosely as she hops. It is also apparent that she is going to deliver a litter of kittens within the next month, and she is currently in the company of a kitten that appears about four months old. The Traveler is down on her luck and needed somewhere to go and someone to help her.

I don't know why she came to our farm or how far she traveled. I don't know how she'll provide for her upcoming family or care for the kitten she has with her. I don't know if she'll stay or move on when the weather is warmer. But somewhere deep down in my heart, I understand her story. She's afraid and desperate and very much alone. She wants to trust and she wants to be loved. I can see it in her eyes and in her cautious attempts to approach me. Should she decide to stay, I will do my level best to care for her. Only the passage of time can write the rest of her story.

I've seen the face of the Traveler many times in my life. It's been reflected in the eyes of people I meet on a daily basis. They are sojourners who feel down on their luck, unloved and afraid. Like the Traveler, they all long for security, acceptance and belonging. Like the Traveler,

The Traveler

they practice wariness because they don't want to be hurt again. Just think of the difference a kind word, a meal or a hand extended out to the finger tips in friendship could make. The Traveler has reminded me of something very important. I can make a difference in the lives of others, even if it's momentary. Every effort, even if unacknowledged, is worth it. Thanks, Traveler, for finding me.

Traveler's Gift

Several months ago I shared with you the story of the Traveler who appeared in the barn in early December. At that time I had no way to predict what the outcome of her presence with us would come to mean. Over the past six months, she has made herself part of our little family and although wary at times, she is happy to be petted and loved. She has expectant eyes when I walk into the barn and can hardly wait for a chin rub. I am pleased with how our relationship has grown into a companionship.

My precious mother died suddenly on April 10. Overcome by grief on that day, I had a sleepless night filled with tears and sadness. The next morning, my husband graciously got up earlier than he normally would and went out to the barn to feed the animals. I just couldn't motivate myself to even rise to meet the new day. Quietly, when he returned from the barn, he entered the bedroom, leaned over, and whispered, "Traveler has delivered a kitten and it's beautiful."

Amidst all the grief, a little spark of new life penetrated the sadness. Mom loved the animals, and she would have been out in the barn to welcome the new arrival. I crawled out of bed, got dressed, and headed to the barn. Traveler was happy to greet me and anxious to be fed. As I shined the flashlight on the new baby, I had to agree with my husband that the kitten was beautiful. Black and gold stripes covered the kitten's body. But I couldn't bring myself to touch the baby. My thoughts were focused on Mom's death. I was filled with sadness.

That evening at chore time, another kitten had been delivered. This time I couldn't help myself; I lay down on the hay and petted Traveler as she nursed her new family. But I still couldn't bring myself to touch the kittens. Unbelievable as it may seem, the next morning there was one more kitten. Traveler had delivered a family of three babies. They were all beautiful and as I lay on the hay talking to her and petting her, she rolled over on her back holding her nursing family with her good leg and her broken leg showing me how proud she was of her family. I cried as I petted the kittens. I was thinking about my mom and dad and my two brothers and myself. Mom had three babies, too. She was proud of each and every one of us. Traveler had reminded me of something very special. Mom had great love for us all.

The Traveler has not found it necessary to hide her kittens and purrs up a storm when her babies are petted. When I lay in the hay, she rises and rubs her nose on mine. It seems we have become partners in raising her new family. All of her fears appear to have vanished as we fuss over the kittens together. Even my husband has become involved. He talks with the Traveler daily and removes his gloves to give the little family a gentle rub. It is still my hope that she will stay with us and I will have an opportunity to welcome her into our house. She's a good mom just like mine was.

It is hard for me to believe that in the dead of winter a sojourner named Traveler came to live at our farm, and in the darkness of my grief she delivered new life that tore the shroud of sadness and gave me hope. Her willingness to share her family with me is amazing. I am confident that my mom would have wanted it this way. Mom knew how much I love the animals. She understood that in the quiet moments with the animals, I am drawn closer to my Heavenly Father as I marvel at His creative handiwork. And somehow, by God's grace, all the pieces of the journey have brought this message of hope and peace to my heart: "Mom is in her eternal home and will someday gather us up in her arms again. Mom's love for us is never ending because it is a gift from God." Thank you, Traveler, for being the deliverer of so great a gift.

A Winter Guardian Angel

Now that winter is preparing to take her leave and the sunshine is once again warm on my face, I must tell you about my wintertime guardian angel. You can tease me about it, say it isn't true, but the following story should confirm that I really do have a wintertime guardian angel.

I drive about 90 miles round trip to and from work. This past winter has really been a "bugger" for me on the roadways. I motor along in a front-wheel-drive sedan that is seven years old. It gets pretty good gas mileage and is reasonably comfortable to ride in, but vast amounts of snow can cause me to grit my teeth, pray like mad, and be careful on the highway.

In early December, it snowed and then got really cold. This was followed by more snow and ice, and more cold. Then for a change-up, we received nuisance snow followed by more cold weather. Throw in a couple of heavy storms with five to eight inches of snow, and then a whopper storm of fourteen inches. All of this was followed by more cold. I'm sure you can relate to the events of the past four months.

The freeway is not always cleared when I merge on at 6:15 a.m. Some of the semi-trucks have buried me in white-out conditions in the darkest hours of the morning. I'm a good driver and have hundreds of thousands of miles behind the wheel, but when alone in the car on treacherous roads, my anxiety has a tendency to rise to fearful levels. When this happens, I hang onto the steering wheel for dear life and pray out loud. I call it a "white-knuckle" drive. On several occasions, I have felt as though I burned up all of my energy for the day driving the 45 miles into work.

On one particularly dangerous morning, with heavy snow falling, I merged onto the freeway behind a green short-box Chevy truck. When I looked in the rearview mirror, there appeared to be about 25 cars, single file, behind me following the Chevy truck. My guardian angel must keep the truck in a garage because the tail lights were bright and clear as we headed up the freeway at 35 miles per hour. Semi-trucks flew by and the road disappeared, but the tail lights on the Chevy were visible. We came upon a terrible accident that I couldn't see up ahead. The Chevy's warning flashers appeared and we all proceeded carefully. At Spirit Mountain the road was a sheet of ice; cautiously and carefully the Chevy truck led our string of cars down into Duluth. I was so grateful, I almost cried when the Chevy took the exit to the Bong Bridge and I continued on to the college in Duluth.

The amazing thing is that this is not a one-time event. On several dangerous mornings when I merged onto the freeway, I found myself behind the Chevy truck. I don't always leave home at the same time. I could be 15 minutes early or 10 minutes late. Still, the Chevy truck would appear leading the way to Duluth. After three successful trips following the truck in horrible weather, I became determined to get close enough to wave to the driver when the roads were clear and dry. Interestingly enough, I never saw the Chevy truck on those mornings, just on the mornings when I was nervous and afraid of the road conditions.

I have fantasized about the driver of the Chevy and where he or she might work over in Superior. I have looked for the truck in my local area at restaurants and gas stations. I have wondered over and over how it could be that the Chevy continued to appear when I needed it most. My best guess is that my guardian angel drives a green short-box Chevy truck in the winter to lead me to safety and calm my fears. It's really too bad because we've been a Ford family my whole life, and I might have to rethink my position about four-wheel drive Chevy trucks. One thing I know…I am grateful for the angel at the wheel.

Leaving the Nest

In late June a pair of barn swallows moved into the old barn and started to build a mud nest on top of one of the bare bulb barn light fixtures. Their craftsmanship was amazing, and I appreciated all of the chicken feathers they had swooped off the lawn to line their nest with. Within a week, the momma bird was sitting on eggs.

I didn't disturb them and really did enjoy their antics in the barn. The horses were undisturbed by their presence and would stand for hours while the pair swooped throughout the entire barn snatching bugs in the air. In July, the babies hatched. I wasn't sure how many were in the nest but their mom and dad spent frantic days gathering food and delivering it to the little peepers.

Leaving The Nest

Every time I was in the barn, I would stand and watch the nest as the birds fed their babies. The horses also stood silently close to the nest location undisturbed by all of the swooping. I think we all were waiting to see the origin of all the little peeping sounds in the barn.

Finally I got a head count. Four tiny beaks were sticking out of the chicken feather nest their mom and dad had created for them. As the days passed, the babies grew and Mom and Dad needed more food for their family, so I opened the side door on the barn that faces the house and locked it open. I spent several minutes each day staring out the living room window watching the swallows "dive bomb" bugs in mid-air and return to the barn to feed their little family.

Finally, the day came when I noticed the little nest was too small for the babies. They had most of their feathers and were sort of stacked up on top of each other in the nest. I knew they would be leaving soon, and I was going to miss them. A few days later when I went out to the barn, the nest was empty and Mom and Dad were gone. I have to admit I was a little sad because I had enjoyed their company for many weeks, and they had vanished without my being able to thank them and wish them luck in their little bug eating lives. I closed the side door on the barn and walked back to the house.

I thought about my children and when they flew the nest. I thought about how hard it was for me to move them out of our home and into apartments. I thought about how their dad and I worked hard to raise them and provide for them. I thought about endless nights of prayer on their behalf and about the good choices they have made in their lives. And I thought about my four precious grandchildren who are in a nest with my daughter and her husband. I still get to be the momma swallow occasionally and look after the babies while they grow their feathers and prepare to take flight.

After a few days, I realized that my little swallow family had moved on just like I had done when my girls grew up and flew the nest of our home. On the third day, I open the side door of the barn and stepped in. There on the top board of the stall stood four little swallows underneath the light fixture and mud nest that had been their home. We all stood silent for a moment, and then they flew around me and out

Leaving The Nest

the door. Little did I know they had been out for flying lessons and would return so I could have a final look at my little mud nest peepers. I was thrilled to see them one more time, and actually I was proud of them. They are off the nest and doing well and I had the opportunity to see them go.

In September, many children and grandchildren leave the nest and head for college. It can be a difficult transition for some barn swallow parents and grandparents like me. I guess I believe you have to trust the flying lessons, pray continually for the peepers, and celebrate their ability to soar. They will return just to show you how well they can really fly.

Beaver Battle

We've lived here on the farm for the past 35 years. Of all the ups and downs during those years, there are a few incidents that stand out as monumental. One of them involves my husband's never-ending battle with the beaver that lived with us for almost all of the 35 years.

The presence of the beaver started out small in the early years of our marriage. They engineered a substantial dam on the back end of our property, creating a pond that brought in weary wildlife for a rest in the spring and fall. Many a morning geese could be seen flying overhead heading for the pond on the back of our acreage. We actually enjoyed hiking to the pond and gazing in wonder at the little paradise the beaver had created.

Beaver Battle

But as our family started to grow, so did the beaver family. Although our house remained the same size, the beavers began to expand their territory. The battle began one summer day when my husband headed out to cut firewood. Fifty big trees were down and the trail was blocked. There was water everywhere making the trail impassable. The beaver had now successfully flooded 30 acres of land right in the middle of our property.

My husband fretted over the best way to force the beaver out for years. Being that dynamite is no longer available like it was when he was a child, his best bet was to continually tear down the dam in hopes that they would retreat to some other spot where their home and dam could reside in peace. In other words, he intended to irritate them into submission, kind of like being married.

He had a grappling hook made, attached it to the tractor and was able to pull down sections of the dam. But, the beavers saw this as a challenge. They called in their best engineer and within 12 hours repairs were made and the water level was back up. Week after week the dam was pulled down in several areas, and week after week it was repaired. Brilliant as beavers are, they even figured out how to flood the high ground where the tractor was used to dismantle the dam. They had thwarted his efforts yet again.

Out of desperation, my husband headed to the dam with the iron rake. He stood on the dam and began to pull it apart. Please note that the dam is about 200 yards long. He punched one hole in the dam and then another. Water was running as he stood watch while he worked. He was going to dry out the beaver.

In one particularly thickly limbed area of the dam, he broke the handle off the rake and, in frustration, threw it out in the woods. He came back to the house to fix the rake and return to the dam, but had to wait till daylight the next day. Filled with determination, he headed out to the dam with the repaired rake. Wonder of wonders. When he returned to the heavily limbed portion of the dam it had been repaired…and sticking out of the repaired area was the broken handle of the rake.

My husband conceded the battle. The beaver had triumphed. Interestingly enough, they moved on within the next two years. The remains of the dam still stand but all of the water is gone. And the rake handle…it's still in the dam. A constant reminder of when to call it quits and let things be.

Save the Last Dance for Me

When I was a little girl, our house was filled with music. My dad had a substantial collection of 78 albums featuring all of the Big Bands. Glen Miller and Tommy Dorsey were household favorites, and frequently while the music was playing on our little record player my dad would ask my mom for a dance. They could swing dance and waltz up a storm. I loved to watch and dreamed of one day being able to dance with Dad like Mom did.

When I was 12, our family vacationed at a resort that had a large dining room, and a small combo band played nightly for dancing. My dad attempted to teach me to dance, and as he did, I walked all over his size 12 shoes while we were on the dance floor. I was so embarrassed I retreated to our table in shame. The rest of the evening I sat and watched Mom and Dad move across the dance floor with grace and beauty and wished that someday I would be able to dance with Dad the way Mom did.

Throughout my parents 68 years of marriage they have frequented every Big Band revival concert that they possibly could and during the past five years have enjoyed the music sitting in their seats with tapping toes. The passage of time and advancing years has left mom frail and unable to join her favorite dance partner on the dance floor. I feared all opportunity had passed for me to be the princess and dance with the king of swing to some of the greatest music ever performed.

I was reading the mail in November and came across an ad for a Veterans Day dance at a nearby location. The Boss Big Band from Duluth was going to appear and provide a variety of music including Big Band. I called Dad and asked him for a date. I would take him to supper and then on to the dance. He should brush off his best bow tie and be prepared because I expected a dancing lesson. Then I called my youngest daughter and made arrangements for her to join us for dinner and dancing.

Save The Last Dance For Me

She is an excellent dancer, and she jumped at the opportunity to dance with her grandpa. We all got gussied up and met for an evening of dinner and dancing.

When I picked Dad up for our date, he was smiling and looked so dapper in his white shirt and red bow tie. We leisurely enjoyed our dinner and conversation, and he stated how proud he was to be out with two of the most beautiful girls in the world. The waitress remarked how wonderful we all looked and suggested she take our picture. Ear-to-ear smiles filled with excitement were reflected in the photo. Following supper, we headed off to the ballroom filled with anticipation. Dad reveled in the music, and when a waltz started to play, he leaned over and asked me to dance. I stayed off his shoes this time and suddenly I realized I was finally having the moment I had waited over 40 years for…I was the princess dancing with the king of swing.

Anna danced with her grandpa several times, and when the "Boogie Woogie Bugle Boy of Company B" was played, they were flying across the floor smoothly and with precision. As I sat and watched, I had to blink back the tears because she looks like Mom and moves like Mom on the dance floor. It was a moment packed with a lifetime of memories. I started to get a little emotional but laughed out loud when Dad said the swing dancing made him sweat.

Time moves too rapidly when you are enjoying every minute of it. Toward the end of the evening, Dad turned to me and said, "let's dance." He had saved the last dance of the evening for me. Like a 12-year-old girl I took his hand, but as his grown daughter I danced the final waltz with my dad. Cinderella and the king moved easily across the floor, enjoying the music and the ease at which they danced together.

As I drove Dad home, he thanked me for the wonderful evening. He said he had forgotten all about his worries and woes for a few hours and enjoyed every minute of our big night out. He raved about our supper and the sound of the Big Band. He was happy and I felt his spirit had been lifted; so had mine.

I tried but couldn't find the words to thank my dad for risking his shoes one more time by asking me to dance. I tried but couldn't find the words to thank Dad for passing on his love of Big Band music. I tried but couldn't find the words to tell him how beautifully he danced with his granddaughter. It was an evening when the dreams of this little girl became reality. I was so choked up when Dad got out of the car that I could only thank him for one thing…saving the last dance for me.

A Leap of Faith

Rion is my four-year-old grandson. He's intelligent, loving, giving and tons of fun. I enjoy every minute I spend with him. His favorite question is "Why?" and that opens the door for learning conversations. He soaks up information like a sponge and is curious about everything. He loves being here on the farm and likes to do chores. Feeding the chickens and throwing hay to the horses is a big deal when you're four years old, and he anxiously awaits the opportunity to be outside with the animals.

A few weeks ago, I had a lot of cleanup to do in the barn, and Rion's mom came to help me put things in order. Rion and his three-year-old sister were in the barn with me while I straightened and stacked my gardening supplies and raked the floor. I made a drum set out of plastic pots, and Rion found some garden stakes and started to play the drums and sing. I sang "Twinkle, Twinkle" and "You Are My Sunshine" while Rion and his sister beat the bottoms of the pots like jazz artists. There was a significant amount of dancing included in our musical rendition of the songs, and the hoopla in the barn brought my huge gelding Laddie into the free stall out of curiosity. Laddie nodded his head and watched us, wishing he could be a part of the band.

There are two six-foot panels that divide the free stall from the rest of the barn. Rion and his sister went over to the bucket of brushes and each grabbed one. Then like monkeys they climbed the panels to brush Laddie's face and neck. I gave stern instructions not to climb any higher than the third rail on the panel and then stood back and watched my grandkids and my horse spend a few minutes together. Both children climbed down and drummed a little more. I got distracted talking with my granddaughter for no more than a heartbeat when out of the corner of my eye I saw Rion on the top rail of the panel with both hands on the center of Laddie's back swinging his little leg over the rail onto the horse. My heart skipped a beat, and instantly I had Rion by the seat of his Wranglers and down standing next to me on the floor. Laddie would not have hurt Rion, but it's a long fall from the top of that big horse.

How is it that at four years old a child can be so fearless and trusting? Rion took a leap of faith swinging his little leg over the top rail. It never occurred to him that he would be anything but safe. There are several things I don't do in my life because I'm scared. Sometimes I don't reach out to others for fear of rejection. Sometimes it's easier to say no than it is to step up and try something new. Sometimes I walk away from a situation when I know I should have held my ground. I've reconsidered my position and my fears and will borrow some of Rion's courage to push forward in faith.

By the way, I became highly motivated after my experience with Rion. Currently, there is a pony and a pony saddle here on the farm, and pony rides are given upon request. When Rion's balance is better, I will put him up on Laddie and the three of us will go for a ride. But in the meantime, I'll just keep practicing Rion's example of swinging my leg over the rail without fear, and trusting in the outcome.

The Christmas Tree

The holidays are upon us. Most of you probably have your homes decorated for Christmas and the New Year. There is a lot to do during December. Attending Christmas concerts, Christmas parties, and assorted church activities barely scratch the surface of holiday celebrations. Christmas baking plus the shopping and wrapping of gifts fill the schedule up to the brim. Throw in a couple of family gatherings and visiting with friends, and December suddenly becomes packed with activities. That's why I hedged on setting up a Christmas tree last year.

We have always had a fresh-cut tree for Christmas. Some years the tree came off our own property. Some years it was a gift from my mom and dad. Sometimes it came from a tree lot. But here on the farm, discussion of an artificial tree was squelched at every turn in the road. In our home, there is something about the smell of a fresh-cut tree that makes it feel like Christmas. Last year I viewed it as too much work. I decided we could do without until I told my grown children there would be no Christmas tree when they came home to celebrate Christmas. A combination of guilt and resolve filled my soul when I told my husband on December 20th that we had to get a tree. No one had trees left at the lots in our area, so my husband and I got a wild idea late in the afternoon to drive to a tree farm and get a tree.

We are not young, and I thought I'd lost my mind when we found the owner of the tree farm at his home. He mentioned our tardiness in procuring a tree and told us we could cut our own but would have to drive our truck back to the tree farm through the front 80 acres of his property. He explained that the trail was very narrow and hilly and we should be mindful of the pines alongside the trail. Filled with foolhardiness, we trundled down the path in our rear-wheel drive pickup. To say the trail was rough was an understatement. The pines he spoke of

The Christmas Tree

were huge trees with barely enough clearance for the truck. I thought we were going to rip the side view mirrors off the vehicle. I was terrified.

After getting stuck several times, the trail opened up and there in the snow stood the prettiest rows of Christmas trees. We spent more than an hour laughing and crunching through the snow until we found the perfect tree. It was cut with a yell of "timber" and loaded into the truck, and my husband gave me a kiss and said, "This feels like Christmas."

I was very concerned about our traveling back down the winding narrow trail in the dark. But, he assured me, we would make it. We always have. After 33 years, why should this journey be any different? We got stuck twice driving out, but he was right…we made it.

Did you know trees look smaller in their natural habitat? I didn't realize the majestic size of our tree until we attempted to bring it into the house. It filled up one end of the living room. I had to buy extra lights to decorate it. It was the most glorious tree we have ever had in our home. The house was filled with the wonderful smell of pine on Christmas morning when our family all arrived. Everyone commented on the

Under The Pine Boughs

beautiful tree, and they were very appreciative that I had reconsidered. So was I.

Sometimes life gets so busy that I hesitate to do the things that bring significance to it. I get overwhelmed with the "have to do list," and relinquish the things that make life so special. This year there will be a tree. Underneath it will be the 34-year-old manger scene that signifies the birth of Christ the Savior. Mary and Joseph will be huddled around the manger where Jesus lays, and the wise men and shepherds will be there, too. Of course, the sheep have a prominent spot, especially the little black one that often reminds me of myself. And, the house will smell of pine. Our family will celebrate once again the true meaning of Christmas, and we'll do it gathered around the tree.

I hope this year you find that special place where the true meaning of Christmas fills your heart and soul with joy. A very Merry Christmas to you and yours and a wish for a Happy New Year filled with hope.

Laddie and the Lost Shoe

⤺

For those of you who have been reading my column for several years, you know that I love to horseback ride. You also know that I own a big eight-year-old palomino gelding (16.1 hands) named Laddie. He is my buddy and traveling companion. We have enjoyed the countryside in Minnesota, Wisconsin, and Iowa for the past five years. My relationship with Laddie is so special that words pale and flounder when I try to explain our partnership and trust. He knows me and all of my faults and yet responds with a willing spirit and open mind to the challenges we face together. I appreciate him and he respects me.

Last July, four days after I had my hand and elbow reconstructed, Laddie was seriously injured in an accident. Both of us were stitched up, me on my right arm, and he on his left foreleg. Recovery for the both of us has been painful and slow. I spent months in occupational therapy, and Ladd spent months in a paddock waiting for green grass and some running room. I fared better, but spring this year found Ladd continuing to limp at the trot.

I had wrestled with his injury mentally and emotionally for almost a year when a knowledgeable veterinarian suggested that I have Ladd shod with a bar shoe to protect his foot. You can't imagine my surprise when, after one week of wearing the shoe, he was sound. I was so excited I called everyone I knew to share with them the miracle of the shoe and then... he lost it somewhere out in the pasture, and I spent three days walking the pasture with a big magnet trying to find it. I never did find it, and Ladd was lame again.

A week later, I had Ladd shod with a set of orthopedic "dancing shoes" and within a couple of days he was sound again. I decided (on a whim) to take him to Wisconsin for a "walking trail ride" and he was wonderful. I enjoyed his company and he was outstanding on the trail. The day before we were to come home, we decided to do a two-hour ride in the late afternoon after a rain storm. Over hill and dale, through mud and water we traveled, and close to the end of the ride Ladd started to limp. I was devastated when I realized he had lost the shoe off his sore foot.

When we got back to camp and Ladd was settled in for the night, I asked one of my fellow campers to give me a ride back to the place where the road crossed the trail. I had a nagging feeling that the shoe was resting in the red clay mud hole we had picked our way through on the trail. Instantly I had three volunteers who would go look for the shoe with me. Then I prayed out loud and asked God to help us find the shoe.

Guess what…I didn't find the shoe but my girlfriend did. It was in the red clay mud hole we had ridden through earlier in the day. We were only in the mosquito-infested woods for about five minutes when she yelled, "I found it!" I was so overwhelmed I cried.

Ladd has his shoe back on and he still has a slight limp. He'll be spoiled rotten until he's feeling better because he is my good friend. I will never doubt that God is interested in every aspect of my life again. He led me to the place of the lost shoe and helped my girlfriend find it. They say miracles don't happen anymore. Well, I believe in them, and the found shoe is just a small example of what a little bit of faith can do when you're looking for something as trivial as a horse shoe. I am awed, humbled, and grateful that my prayer was answered. Someday soon Ladd and I will be back on the trail together, and I'm convinced I really never ride alone. God's eye is on the sparrow, and I know He watches me.

Till the Cows Come Home

I think I've heard the phrase, "till the cows come home," hundreds of times in my lifetime. As I recall, it was consistently used as a metaphor for a job that was going to take nearly forever to complete. This is probably due to the fact that cows have a wayward spirit about the grass always being greener on the other side of the fence. And, unless there's milking to be done, the cattle roam until someone goes out to fetch them.

We raised beef cattle for 20 years, and I can attest to the fact that fence repair was a top priority spring, summer, fall, and winter. I marveled when the calves were born at their ability to slip through the fence to find a cool spot to nap and at their ability to slip back into the pasture at mother's call to move on with the herd. Yearly, in the spring, our small herd would leave the comforts of home to visit with the neighbors. I would walk down the road and call "come on," and they would lift their heads, answer me and follow me home. But one year they slipped through the fence and wandered so far they were lost.

After morning chores, I had taken our daughters to a doctor's appointment in Duluth. I returned home close to two o'clock in the afternoon and the cows were gone. It was cold outside and the ground was frozen. There was a small amount of snow left in the woods, but from my quick survey of the situation there were no tracks to follow. I telephoned my parents for help, and Mom stayed with our children while Dad and I headed out to find the cows.

Dad went due east across our property carrying a bucket of grain; and I headed northeast in a similar fashion. Deep in the woods about a half mile from home, I picked up the tracks of what could only be our herd. I walked another mile through the woods and finally spotted the herd 100 yards ahead on an open ridge. I called "come on" and shook the bucket. One head turned to look and I called again. I heard the bawl of our oldest cow and I believe she looked at me in relief and headed my way. They were lost and wanted me to lead them home.

I was cold to the bone, and my labored breath left clouds of mist in the air. The cows came running and we turned and headed back through the woods. The sun was down, but a few streaks of light on the west horizon guided me toward home with the cows and calves in single file behind me. They say cattle can't be moved at night, but our little herd followed me all the way back to our property in the dark, through the gate, and back to the barn.

My father had returned to the house several hours earlier and paced the farm yard worried about me and the herd. In the dark he heard me coming, calling "come on" and answered me with "you're home." Funny thing...we fixed the fence the next day, and the cows stayed home for a long time.

In retrospect, I think at times we all wander to where we think the grass is greener on the other side of the fence. Sometimes we lose our way and are far from a place of comfort and love. Sometimes we find our way home, and sometimes someone has to look for us calling "come on" and lead us toward home. Home really isn't a building or a piece of property. It's more of a feeling of being loved, safe, accepted, and comforted. You carry that feeling in your heart. No matter your situation, I hope today finds you coming up the well-worn path to the place you call home.

The Sugar Incident

Over the past two years I've been sharing little snippets of my life experiences with you. You've met some of my dearest friends and walked with me through some of my crazier moments. I had an experience this past week that was so challenging and funny I just have to share it with you.

I did a fair amount of baking for the holidays in November and December. I like the way the house smells when there are cookies in the oven, and Christmas just wouldn't be complete without homemade fudge. I bake a lot. Whenever our family gathers you can find me in the kitchen stirring up something sweet that I hope everyone will enjoy. I try to keep the pantry well stocked. The pantry in my kitchen is really a lower cupboard with two good-sized shelves that house my baking supplies. And sometimes I've been known to forget items that have inadvertently slipped to the rear of the cupboard.

Well, I was going to make an apple pie, and the sugar canister was close to empty. I was sure I had another five pound bag in the pantry that I could use to fill the canister. So I got down on my hands and knees in the kitchen and rummaged through the bottom shelf of the cupboard. There it was way in the back and as I lifted it up, I realized it was rock hard. I did a quick mental assessment and came to the conclusion that this bag must have been purchased this past summer and escaped to the back of the cupboard when I was filling the pantry with the items I used for my holiday baking.

Not to be undaunted in my baking pursuit, I made a quick decision to slam the bag on the kitchen floor to break up the sugar. I'm not sure if I saw someone do this at some time in my life or if it just seemed like the best approach to my dilemma. So I took the bag and slammed it on the floor. Nothing happened. Seeing my efforts as weak, I tried again. This time I put a little

The Sugar Incident

more muscle into it and, wham, the bag burst open and sugar was all over the kitchen floor.

I ranted briefly about sugar bags not being what they once were but became totally distracted when my dog came sailing into the kitchen and started to lick up the sugar like a machine. You realize I'm still on my knees, and the more I push the dog away the more the sugar gets distributed throughout the kitchen and dining room. I went to get the broom to start the cleanup but the sugar just kept spreading. I put the dog out, and that process alone brought the sugar onto the back porch. I was standing in the middle of the mess with a broom trying to decide what my best approach would be when I burst out laughing.

Sometimes I take life too seriously and it takes a "sugar incident" to snap me back into really living in the moment and being at peace with it. Oh yes, I did get my kitchen, dining room, and porch cleaned up. I only had to wash the floor twice to get rid of the stickiness. And the apple pie was wonderful.

My advice...enjoy today, laugh at yourself, and never slam a rock hard, five-pound bag of sugar on the floor unless you're prepared to deal with the consequences.

Moose Lake State Hospital

I have had the unique blessing of teaching at the College of St. Scholastica for the past twelve years. Over the semesters, I've had hundreds of students in the class-room, some of which are so intelligent and eager to learn that being their professor has been humbling. I regularly challenge my students to pick internships that will expand their knowledge base and hopefully help them become competent in areas of weakness. Last semester I challenged a group of students to volunteer some of their time aiding individuals with developmental disabilities. It was the first time a student turned to me and said, "I'm afraid." Immediately, I remembered a time when I was afraid, and I shared with her the following life story.

When I was seventeen, we moved from the Twin Cities to small town Minnesota when my father accepted the call to serve three small country Lutheran churches as their pastor. If the truth were known, I was dead set against the move. I resented having to leave my home and friends and my high school at the end of my junior year. I never wanted to graduate from small town Barnum with a bunch of unknown students. I wanted my friends and the hubbub of the Cities. And, I never wanted to be a pastor's kid.

Despite being resentful, I was dutiful and made the move to northern Minnesota. On a cold November Sunday, my dad asked me to go with him and my mom to the Moose Lake State Hospital to provide a service for the developmentally disabled people who lived there. He wanted me to bring my guitar and provide the music for the chapel service. I was petrified. But Dad assured me all would be well as we got into the car.

Upon our arrival at the state hospital, I had a sense of resolve and felt fine until we walked through the security doors. Mom and Dad checked us in, and we walked down a long corridor toward the chapel. Suddenly out of nowhere came a small man wearing a labeled hard hat that read "Crabby." He leaped at my dad and crawled up my dad's six foot four frame, swung his legs around my dad's waist and hugged the stuffing out of my dad. My dad continued to walk down the hall, and soon several men were holding onto my dad's arms and legs as we made our way to the chapel. My mom was wearing a camel-colored coat with a large fur collar, and two women had snuggled under my mom's arms to walk to the chapel.

I was scared to death. I had my guitar case firmly in hand, and when anyone got near me I positioned the case so that I would remain untouched. I felt like I'd been thrown into the deep end of the pool and couldn't manage this new situation. I was in an environment I didn't understand, and I was overwhelmed. Then it happened.

I sat on a small stage, so I could play my guitar in safety. My dad stood right in front of the patients that had gathered and gave a very simple devotional. Repeatedly, Crabby got up and hugged my dad. My mom sat in the middle of the front row with her arms around a precious woman with dark brown hair who was enamored with the collar of Mom's coat. Several times she kissed my mom, and my mom gently stroked her arm and held her close.

I played several well known hymns without much participation from the crowd, and then Dad asked me to play Jesus Loves Me. A chorus of voices erupted in the little chapel as we sang it over and over again. My fear evaporated. These wonderful people had gathered with us. Their hearts were bursting with love and kindness, and I had been too afraid to accept it.

Crabby helped me carry my guitar to the front door of the hospital. He crawled up my dad's frame one more time for a hug. The dark-haired woman cried when my mom hugged her goodbye, and I left the Moose Lake State Hospital a different person. My narrow understanding had been expanded, and I'd had a change of heart. Love really does cast out all fear, and I'd been loved by a precious group of people.

Dad and Mom set a great example for me on that cold November Sunday thirty-eight years ago. The experience changed me so completely that my education and career has involved working with people who deal with a variety of psychological handicaps. So when my student told me she was afraid, I had a measure of understanding about her fear. I told her it would be all right. I'd go with her.

The Little Yellow Dress

Inside a heavy cardboard box, wrapped in layers of tissue paper, on the top shelf of the storage shelves in the basement of my childhood home was a little yellow dress. When I was about four years old I thought it was the prettiest dress I had ever seen. Every few years my mother would take the box off the shelf and hand wash and iron the little yellow dress. Lovingly she would wrap it up in layers of tissue paper and pack it back in the box. It wasn't until I was about seven years old that I understood that the dress had been mine.

We moved to a different house when I was twelve and I'd forgotten about the dress. But just before my thirteenth birthday it appeared again in my mother's hands being washed and ironed. We moved again when I was seventeen.

Little did I know the precious yellow dress had made the trip, too.

The years seem to roll by with college and marriage and by the time my first daughter was born, I had no memory of the little yellow dress. But when my mother came to my home with the heavy old cardboard box I knew instantly what was inside. The "Polly Flinders" smocked little yellow dress with the white collar, tiny lace trim, and big bow. It really was the prettiest little dress I had ever laid eyes on. My mom passed on to me the responsibility of the treasure that I had once worn on my first birthday.

My daughter wore the dress to church on her first birthday. She looked so precious I wished I could freeze the moment in time forever. My mother was beaming that Sunday. All the years of care and protection brought back a moment for her of when I was just a toddler. She said her granddaughter was just as beautiful as I had once been when I wore the dress. I thanked my mom a thousand times over for saving the little yellow dress for all of those years. We both cried a lot that day. As the years passed, my daughter grew up into a fine young woman,

The Little Yellow Dress

went to college, fell in love, got married, and started a family of her own.

When my granddaughter was born I carefully opened my hope chest. Nestled close to the bottom, wrapped in tissue paper, was the little yellow dress. I washed and ironed it and presented it to my daughter. It was still just as pretty as it was all those years ago when I wore it for the first time. I explained to my daughter that this dress had been mine and her grandma had saved it for me to pass on to her. She had worn it on her first birthday and now it was time for me to pass it along to her for my granddaughter.

Just before my granddaughter's first birthday, my daughter appeared at my home with a package for me. Inside was a professional photograph of my precious granddaughter wearing the little yellow dress. My heart was so full I thought it would burst. The dress my mother had so carefully cared for, the dress I had hidden in the hope chest was being worn by the most beautiful little girl in the world. I now know how my mother felt when her granddaughter wore the dress for her first birthday. But, this story really isn't about the little yellow dress.

It's about the love of a mom for her daughter. It's about protecting and carefully handling that love, and it's about preserving that love for future generations.

I went to see my mom at the dementia assisted living home where she currently lives, and I gave her a copy of the photo of her great-granddaughter. She looked at it for a long time and turned to me and said, "What a beautiful baby in a beautiful dress." Yes, Mom, the love in our family continues, and you were a wonderful example of how to nurture and pass down that love to future generations. Thanks, Mom, for showing me what it means to be a mother and a grandmother. And, thanks, Mom, for saving the little yellow dress.

Murphy's Law

Murphy's Law states that if anything can go wrong it probably will. For the past two days I've been studying Murphy's Law and the experience has been so overwhelmingly funny I thought I should share it with you.

On a recent rainy day I intended to capture some informational forms off the internet that I needed to complete a project. Please understand that I live way out in the country and currently our computer is only hooked to the Internet via a dial-up connection. This project should have only taken a micro minute to complete, and after two hours of struggle I was mentally kicking my computer around our home office. I did finally get the job done but not without high levels of frustration.

Under The Pine Boughs

As a reward for tenacity, I drove the five miles to our local country store to gas up my car and to mail off some letters. I took my dog "Max" along for the ride. He likes to stand between the front seats in the car and watch the road while I drive. He smiles and wags his tail when we go for a ride, and I thought it was just the tension reliever I needed after my computer experience. When we got to the store I pulled up to the pump and told Max to get in the back seat, and I got out of the car. Max jumped back into the front seat, jumped to the driver's door, and locked himself in the car with my purse, cell phone, and car keys. I froze looking at his happy face while I felt my hair start to melt. I think I ran around the car twice. It wasn't helpful but it did relieve a little anxiety. I went into the store and tried to call someone but no one, and I mean no one, was home. Finally, the store owner tossed me his car keys so I could run home and get my extra set. Max enjoyed his stay at the gas pumps. He wagged his tail and smiled at everyone who came and went from the store. When I finally got back and opened the door of the car, he couldn't wait for me to start the car and head down the road. I couldn't believe two Murphy moments had occurred in just a few hours. Feeling the need not to touch a thing, I went to bed early and prayed that tomorrow would be a better day.

Morning arrives for me at 5:00 a.m. and my preparations for work were well underway. I left the house with my coffee cup and book bag and drove approximately a quarter of a mile when I realized the car sounded strange. Investigation proved my deepest fears when the passenger rear tire turned up flat. I turned around and carefully drove home. My husband met me at the door with a solution. He would drive me to work and get the tire fixed later in the day. I was relieved as I grabbed my coffee cup and book bag and climbed into the truck. I extolled my thanks for him being my "knight in shining armor" and settled into the seat for the ride. I haven't ridden in the truck for some time and all was well for the first few miles. Did you know travel mugs should really have their caps on when you ride in a truck? I had long since forgotten but when we hit the first bump in the road and I was suddenly wearing my coffee, I experienced a sincere longing for a travel mug cap.

The rest of the day progressed well and when I finally arrived home in the evening, I phoned my brother in an effort to catch-up. As I described to him the events of the past two days he laughed till he cried and suggested I change my career and become a stand-up comic. I burst out laughing.

Life can be pretty funny and exasperating at the same time. I did, however, after much thought, find the solution to Murphy's Law. It's hope. And hope can squelch Murphy in all circumstances. Hope helped get the forms off the Internet, the extra set of car keys, the ride to work, and the coffee stains out of my dress shirt. Hope is optimism at its best. I'm doing my best to practice it. How about you?

Beaunitta

I've been a member of our local parish for a number of years and have had the privilege of participating in the "children's moments" for thirteen of those years. Once every month I prepare a teaching moment based on the Biblical reading for that particular Sunday and share it during the service with the small children and adults in attendance. The experience for me has been unique and wonderful. I've been allowed the liberty to parallel tangible objects with scripture, and sometimes my illustrations have been uncommon experiences for all in attendance including me. Several examples of the living object lessons would have included: my beagle who sang along with the organ, the baby chicks that almost escaped, the rooster who crowed outside the church but was quiet inside, and a cat. Several examples of other objects would have included: a shovel, a life vest, a canoe paddle, birthday cake, a lantern, a saddle, bubbles, and too many more items to enumerate. But one particular Sunday about a year ago was so unique I thought I should share it with you.

Several times over the years I have used horse equipment as object lessons for the "children's moment." Because I am a horse person and do a fair amount of riding, whenever I brought something in that was horse related our pastor would teasingly ask me when I was bringing the horse to church. Well, last year in June I told him I was ready. I'm not sure he thought I was really going to do it, but when my husband and I were at the church early on Sunday morning duct taping indoor/outdoor carpeting to the floor in the front of the church, he got the idea that it was going to happen. I had written a children's moment comparing controlling a horse with a bridle to learning to control our own tongues, or the words we speak to one another. The only difference was that this time after 150 "children's moments" I was anxious. A horse is a big, powerful animal and the unexpected can happen in an instant. Adding to my anxiety was a church filled with people.

Before we brought the horse into the church I asked all the children to come forward and sit quietly in the front pew. There were about 16 kids piled up anxiously waiting for me to begin. They had no idea what was in store until I opened the side door and "Beaunita" started to come through the door. Everyone in the church gasped and then something wonderful happened. She stood quietly by my side in front of the congregation as though she knew this was a time for reverence. Beaunita exuded peace as she looked at all of the people in the church. I laid my hand on her shoulder as I began to share the story, and all of my anxiety evaporated. I closed the "children's moment" with a short prayer and was compelled out of a grateful heart to hug Beaunita. The funny thing is, she hugged me first. When I went to wrap my arms around her beautiful head, she leaned into me and sighed. Our church was filled with a stunned silence.

Beaunita really gave the "children's moment" that Sunday and not me. My interpretation is that it was about trust and peace. The kind of trust and peace that surpasses all understanding. I got the message softly yet very clearly on a Sunday morning at church with a horse.

Remembering Evelyne

Evelyne was a stately dignified woman. Her hair was coiffured in a beautiful style and she wore beautiful clothes. In fact, of the years I knew her, I can't remember a time when she wasn't dressed up. Evelyne never married, and she lived alone in a small house next to the town hall. When our family moved to rural Minnesota, she was one of the first individuals I had the pleasure of meeting. Evelyne was the Post-Mistress of the small town of Mahtowa and she knew everybody. Attached to the post office in town was a small gift store where she sold dry goods and penny candy. Evelyne worked well into her seventies, but it wasn't the post office I will always remember her for; she was the music director and organist at our country church.

Remembering Evelyne

Evelyne played the organ at our church for more than 50 years. Sunday mornings, weddings, and funerals found Evelyne sitting on the organ bench with her shoes off playing preludes, hymns, liturgy, classical music and postludes. Rain or shine, snow or sleet, Evelyne was there. She rarely took vacation and was dedicated to providing music at our church. Her gift of music was a tremendous offering of her faith to God and to all who enjoyed her music year after year. The church hosted a party for Evelyne when her years of donated time and music reached the benchmark of 50 years. Swift hands and swift feet and a heart for music kept Evelyne playing along.

It's a funny thing but it took me almost twenty years to finally understand how valuable Evelyne's faith and contribution were to our church family. Pastors come and go, but a good organist works tirelessly to make sure the services continue. Evelyne kept the services moving along when there were time lapses, interruptions, and mishaps. She could throw in a chorus at any time to give continuity to the worship service. The choir blossomed under her direction with 16 members all trying to out-sing the organ. Her leadership was quiet and stately and everyone who was involved wanted to do a good job when working alongside Evelyne. We didn't want to let her down because she set such a great example of quiet servitude and faith.

Evelyne never looked for recognition. In fact, thanking her almost embarrassed her. On one Easter Sunday I finally understood what motivated Evelyne to keep playing for all of those years. The church was packed with people. Flowering plants were displayed beautifully across the entire front of the church. Every pew and extra chair was filled. Young children and babies were held on laps to make room for more to sit. Standing room was taken, and the congregation spilled out the vestibule and on to the steps. We all stood up to sing the opening hymn "Jesus Christ is Risen Today" and the chorus of voices singing on that Easter morning almost took the roof off the church. Evelyne's hands and feet were flying, and I saw something I had never seen before. Evelyne closed her eyes while playing and a beautiful smile appeared on her face. She was accompanying a great choir, singing praise to the Father of her faith.

Remembering Evelyne

Evelyne died several years ago. I heard she was walking up the stairs to her dentist's office when her heart gave out. In an instant, she was gone. I'd like to believe she was summoned to play the organ in another realm for a much larger congregation. I can almost see her hands flying over the keys of the organ, and I can almost hear a great choir. Evelyne's gift of music and her dedication to her faith are eternal. I am so blessed to have known and experienced this great example of quiet faith and servitude. I miss you, Evelyne, but someday I'll be joining you. I'll be singing in the choir.

Christmas

During the early days of December while preparations are underway for the Christmas season, I find myself reflecting on the Christmases of years gone by. When our daughters were little, the anticipation and excitement about Christmas filled our home with secrets and laughter. The decorating of the tree and baking of cookies were just the beginning of weeks filled with school programs, Sunday school programs, and visits to friends. It was a wonderful time to see through the eyes of the children and to experience the joy of giving to others selflessly. In our home we wanted our girls to understand that always and especially at Christmastime it is far better to give than to receive. One Christmas, almost 20 years ago, taught us all the graciousness of receiving when we were incapable financially of being the givers.

It had been a very difficult year. Everything that could have gone wrong did, and my husband worked endless hours at his job in an effort to keep us afloat. I was sick, so sick I had an IV line installed in my right arm and underwent treatment every day. There wasn't an extra cent in our home that wasn't delegated to one bill or another, and Christmas was coming. I spoke with my extended family and we all agreed that being together was far more satisfying than gift giving. We were doing everything we could to "get by," and we explained the situation to our girls so that there wouldn't be disappointment and tears on Christmas morning.

I baked cookies and my husband found a beautiful tree in our woods that would serve as our Christmas tree. It even came with a nest, which fascinated the girls as we decorated the tree. Outwardly all things appeared normal at our house, but inside I felt empty. The joy of the upcoming holiday was waning, and there was so much I wanted to do but couldn't. I fussed a lot over my inability to give to friends, extended family, and especially my children. The girls needed snow pants and boots. My husband needed winter boots and work gloves. These were needs, and I couldn't even begin to think about the wants of my family. I wrestled silently with all the needs and wants and finally had to let it all go so that I could really celebrate the birth of Christ and be thankful for all I already had. We would be fine. We had each other and enough love in our home to dispel any disappointments and financial hardships. And, duct tape really can fix just about anything and make it last a little longer.

Christmas Eve day finally arrived and at about 4:30 in the afternoon a man I'd never met before knocked on our front door. He had three teenagers with him and they were all wearing Santa hats. I thought they were lost and looking for directions, but he asked if this was the Carlson house and I said yes. Package after package was brought into our home as we stood in stunned silence. Tearfully, I asked him his name and hugged him. He replied, "Santa" and walked out the door and drove away into the night.

On Christmas morning we opened the presents that came from our "Santa." There were snow pants, boots, and rollerblades for the girls, winter boots and gloves for my husband, a 500-piece mystery puzzle for the family, and in the box with my name on it was a wool winter coat. I had never mentioned it and couldn't believe that somehow someone knew how desperately I needed a coat, and it was the right size and just what I would have picked out. We all wrote thank you notes with nowhere to send them. We all worked on the puzzle for a week. We learned about receiving graciously what we could not give ourselves, and we had a fabulous Christmas. Maybe that is the true spirit of Christmas…receiving graciously what we couldn't give ourselves. It came wrapped up in swaddling clothes and lying in a manger on the very first Christmas morning.

Canning

This is the time of year where we complete our "gathering in" here on the farm and reflect on what our "stores" are for winter. The soil has been turned in the garden and cords of split firewood are stacked behind the house. The flower beds are resting and the smell of fall hangs heavy in the air. The shelves in the pantry are laden with canned goods and are a promise of the taste of warm sunshine in the cold dead of winter.

As I was looking at the jars of canned beets, beans, jams, and peaches in the pantry a word came to mind. The word is "sweltering". In late August I stood in the kitchen for days with every pot and pan I own set on boil on the stove. The temperature outside the house was 95 degrees and I think the kitchen (we don't

Canning

have air conditioning) was somewhere around 110 degrees. To swelter is to be overcome by heat and feel as though you might burn up. I actually thought I was going to melt like the wicked witch from the Wizard of Oz. Needless to say that didn't happen, but I do need to add that canning became a spiritual experience for me. Let me explain how this happened.

In July I went to the strawberry fields to pick berries. As I was picking I thought about all of my family members and friends who would enjoy a jar of homemade jam. While I was cleaning and mashing berries and turning them into jam, I thought about each person who would receive a jar and about how much they mean to me in my life and I prayed for each one.

Next came the blueberries. Blueberry jam is an acquired taste and some of the people in my life will drive over just to hear the "ping" of the lid on the jar as it seals. They do this because they know that every jar is a labor of love.

My dad had been admiring the garden all summer and he asked me one day what I was going to do with all the beets. He said he was hoping I'd make some pickled beets like his mom made when he was a boy. In my kitchen pickled beets take a long time to make and as I was putting the filled jars into the hot water bath I thought about my Grandma. She was a wonderful blessing to my life. She died 36 years ago and her influence still rests with our whole family. She was a woman of great faith and she loved her family.

The peaches...well, they were my doing. I have a weakness for fresh produce and I couldn't refuse. This is where the "sweltering" came in. It takes a long time to can a lug of peaches. But their sunny yellow color will bring a smile to everyone in the middle of winter. Not to mention that their taste is pure sunshine. Again the names and faces of friends and family surrounded me as I toiled in my kitchen.

Canning for me isn't about what I have. It's about what I can share. It's not about giving what some might call a "cheap" gift. It's about prayer and love for all of the people who are a part of my life. It's about sunshine and the promise of warm days next spring. It's about laughter and friendship, and about a Creator who has blessed us with wonderful food to eat. Canning really was a spiritual experience for

Canning

me this year, and as I look at all that is in the pantry I am overcome with gratefulness.

One last thought…I can't wait to give my brother his jar of dilly beans this year. There's a lot of red pepper in the recipe. Maybe on a cold winter's night he'll learn what the word "swelter" really means.

Veteran's Day Thanksgiving

It's hard to believe that Thanksgiving is almost here. With the whirlwind of summer and early fall, it seems like the days fly by so fast I hardly get a chance to plan ahead for Thanksgiving. Last year at this time my daughter was deployed with the Air National Guard to the Middle East, and although we still celebrated Thanksgiving the empty chair at our table was a reminder to all of us for how grateful we can be for the men and women who serve our country with courage and faith and how much they are missed by their families and loved ones.

In our home, when someone is missing from a holiday celebration, we set the table as though we expect them to arrive and join us at any minute. Before we sing the table grace, each

Veteran's Day Thanksgiving

person around the table has the opportunity to mention the name of the person they wish could join us. Sometimes the person mentioned is deceased, or deployed, or has been unable to join us for whatever reason. But we still miss their presence. This tradition has gone on for years in our home. I just didn't understand how far reaching this tradition was until my daughter returned from her deployment.

At the base overseas where she was stationed, a similar tradition occurred each day. In the dining room there was a table set for one. Fresh flowers are put on the table each day and the place setting is perfectly prepared as if the President of the United States was going to join our service men and women for a meal. Only the table isn't set for a dignitary or the president; it has been set for the men and women of our armed forces who have died in the line of duty or who are missing in action. It is a somber reflection of the wish that those who were lost were coming home to be with us and share another meal.

When my daughter shared this story with me I felt honored and humbled. I thought about the countless families who would be missing a family member who gave their life for our country. I thought about wives without husbands and husbands without wives. I thought about parents without children and children without parents. I thought about the cost of our freedom and the courage it takes to defend it.

Veteran's Day is Wednesday November 11th and I want to thank all of you who have served this great country in the military. In my family, my dad and six uncles served in WWII, my brother served during Vietnam, and my daughter has served in the Middle East. Not only to my family but to all of you who have served our country in the military, thank you that we can celebrate Thanksgiving. Thank you for the sacrifices you've made on my behalf. Thank you that my grandchildren were born under the stars and stripes of freedom. With great respect and a heart filled with gratitude, I'll be setting the Thanksgiving table with and extra chair and place setting and thanking God for your service and wishing you could join us for a meal of turkey with all the trimmings.

Dot's First Christmas

Dorothy Louise was born into our family in 1994. She arrived with the most beautiful brown eyes you have ever seen and a face that could light up a room. She was about five pounds when we brought her home and gained weight steadily from October till December. She was liver and white in color and really resembled a pig, but she was a Bassett Hound that won over our hearts the day she came home.

Dot (or "Pigger" as we called her) was very well-mannered and a joy to spend time with. She loved dumb-dumb suckers and ice cream and was a natural-born beggar. Her antics were hysterical and everyone loved Dottie.

Dot was about five months old her first Christmas. My husband had carefully selected the perfect tree for our home and set it up in the living room. I have always enjoyed decorating for the holidays, and the house looked beautiful. The tree was outstanding with its lights and decorations. So beautiful it almost took your breath away. Our living room looked like a Norman Rockwell painting. The stockings were hung and Christmas Eve dinner was cooking when our guests arrived. Dottie was the life of the party and stole everyone's heart and attention. After a wonderful dinner with family and friends, (Dottie was under the dining room table) we headed to the local parish for the eleven o'clock Christmas Eve service. Never before had Christmas Eve been so perfect. It was like a Christmas card, picture perfect in every way.

When we came home after the church service the first indication that something was wrong was that there were no lights from the Christmas tree in the front window when we drove into the yard. When we opened the front door the tree was down and the needles were everywhere, but there were no ornaments to be found. On the couch were all the cans from the garbage. Green bean cans from the green bean bake, mushroom soup cans, pineapple cans and table napkins littered the couch. The couch was actually covered with very clean garbage. So clean only a dog could be responsible. In the midst of the garbage slept Dottie. She was guilty, but very happy.

This was the year I learned about forgiveness and that everything need not be perfect for the holidays. It was the year our tree went from pristine to a "Charlie Brown" Christmas tree. This was the year we mounted wood screws into the corner of the living room so we could wire the tree to the wall. This was the year we hunted for the missing ornaments as though they were Easter eggs and found them in every room of the house slightly chewed but well hidden. This was the year we laughed till we cried. This was the year when Christmas no longer looked commercial in our house. It was the start of something more meaningful and deeply satisfying.

Thanks, Dottie for teaching our whole family that Christmas is really about a tiny baby born in a stable. It's about caring and sharing, and it's about peace. Real peace that even a downed tree and broken ornaments can't shatter. And, it's about love. Love for one another and for a brown-eyed pup with a bright smiling face.

Straw Hat

On the top shelf of the bookcase in my living room sits an old straw hat. The hat is several years old. It was never worn as an Easter bonnet. There is nothing fancy about the hat. It is made of yellow straw and has a wide brim and two grommets in the headband where a green ribbon passes through the brim so you can tie it under your chin.

This is a working hat that is well worn from hours in the sunshine. I remember driving to the farm and looking for the hat. Sometimes it would catch my eye from the vegetable garden swinging along with the hoe. Sometimes I would gaze out into the fields and see it atop the tractor and baler. Even the flower garden wasn't complete without the straw hat bobbing up and down when weeding needed to be done.

Occasionally I would spot it resting in the shade with a glass of lemonade right under the brim.

The woman who wore this hat had blue eyes the color of the sky and a smile that could light up an entire room. She was tall and strong and enjoyed the rewards of hard work. I remember her as eternally active, moving from one project to another with the grace of a swan. She milked cows, baled hay, cleaned the barn, grew a huge vegetable garden, tended flowers, baked, cooked, canned, cleaned, mowed grass, raised four children, sewed, quilted, petted the cat, played with her grandchildren, and always had time for her neighbors. And, the straw hat bobbed along in the sunshine with a smile in the shade of the brim.

All of my memories of the straw hat are bathed in sunshine and love. To me it has become a symbol of a life well lived and appreciated. Straw hat had a grateful heart in the midst of adversity. She remained faithful and undaunted whatever the circumstances were. Many times we sang together her favorite hymn "Great is Thy Faithfulness" and because of her example, I went from struggling with my concerns to being thankful for each moment of every day.

Today we struggle with what the future holds. Will there be employment? Will the economy rebound? Will there be money for retirement? Will there be adequate health care? I think the answer lies in the straw hat. I'm going to practice being thankful for every moment of everyday. I'm going to set an example of a life well lived despite my circumstances. I'm going to share happiness with my family and friends. I'm going to dust off the straw hat and wear it this summer while I work in my garden and mow my lawn. You'll know it's me when you drive by. There will be a green ribbon tied under my chin and a smile on my face in the shade of the brim.

Remembering Emma

I met Emma when I was a young mom with two small children in tow. She was a widow, who was in her seventies with silver grey hair and a twinkle in her eye. We were both members of the local parish and we had an attraction for each other like none other. Emma had spirit, and spunk, and an incredible sense of humor. She loved "pussy willows." Emma and I worked on several projects together at the parish and I knew whenever we got together it would be fun. Somewhere in the first few years of our relationship, I forgot how old Emma was. She never seemed to age.

Emma taught me about living. She was kind, and generous. When she saw a need in our community, she rolled up her sleeves and pitched in. She donated boundless amounts of time and energy and never seemed to tire. Emma had a deep inner peace that affected everyone she came into contact with. She was quick with a smile and a laugh, but most of all, she was an encourager.

Emma never had children but she loved mine. She called me every week just to "check in" and see how things were going. She encouraged me in my schooling, parenting, family life, community life, and spiritual life. Whenever I was feeling overwhelmed she'd tell me a funny story, and the laughter we shared would lift my burden.

Then came the cancer, and Emma taught me about dying. Emma had several surgeries, and it was my time to rally around her. I rolled up my sleeves and pitched in. All that I had learned from Emma about living I mobilized into action. I went to see her in the hospital and we laughed to ease the burden. I called her every week at first and then every day. She wasn't afraid to die. She saw death as a graduation from this life to something greater.

I was there the day Emma and the pastor planned her funeral. Emma could no longer eat and was rail thin. To lift our spirits, she told us a funny story about cutting up her charge card because she no longer needed it. Then came my assignment. She said, "At my funeral I don't want you to buy flowers; I want the biggest bouquet of helium balloons you can get in your car and I want you to tie them to the corner of my casket. After the graveside service I want you to cut them loose and be happy."

Emma's sister came to care for her during her final days. I called every day with this message, "tell Emma I love her." On Emma's last day I called but was so emotional I couldn't speak. Her sister graciously said she would give Emma my message. Emma died during the night. When I heard she had died, I cried in secret because Emma wanted me to be happy for her.

I brought the balloons to the funeral. There were so many in my car I could hardly see the road. They kept creeping around in the car. I tied them to Emma's casket just like she had asked. I missed her and her sense of humor. But Emma got me one more time. When the casket was being loaded into the hearse there was a stiff wind blowing and the funeral directors were having a terrible time getting the balloons into the hearse. It was such a funny sight that I burst out laughing. The funeral directors were fighting wild balloons. At the cemetery I cut the balloons loose and watched them fly. One circled back as if waving, and I was filled with gratitude and peace. You see, Emma didn't want the balloons for herself; she wanted the experience for me. Even in her death she was teaching me.

Emma died 17 years ago. Early in the spring, I search the ditch banks for the appearance of the first "pussy willows." They appear sometimes in early February, but almost always by March. They were Emma's favorite. The impact Emma had on my life continues. She so graciously taught me about living and dying in a way she knew I would understand. Every lesson was wrapped in love and encouragement, and seasoned with humor. Thanks, Emma.

My Christmas Story

Many years ago, I decided that my husband and I should host a memorable Christmas experience. We started preparing in July. Steve would build a huge sleigh to be pulled by the tractor that could accommodate 25 people. And I would provide a banquet of food for a dinner party. We set the date for early December and started making our plans.

Despite the fact that we both were working full-time jobs, the sleigh was built and the house was cleaned within an inch of its life. I borrowed tables and chairs, prepared my best linens, washed the wine and water glasses, bought a host of fancy decorations, and shampooed every carpet in the place. We were going to celebrate the festival of lights, and we were so excited we could hardly stand it.

The invitations had gone out and the response was overwhelming. There would be 22 in attendance. Friends and family were coming from all over Minnesota. They were excited to attend. Hotel reservations had been made, and we were headed toward an event I was sure would be enchanting.

It took both of my daughters and me two days to set up for the meal. The prep work was tedious. I wanted everything to be perfect, and for me, it was. When the guests started to arrive, the tree was lit, and the festive atmosphere had everyone smiling. Laughter and joy filled the house as we visited and sat down for a wonderful meal.

When the dishes had been cleared, everyone drew a name from a hat. Written on each card was the name of someone else in the room. The purpose of the name drawing was to offer encouragement to each other in a very intimate setting. Tears were shed, and there was a spirit of love and support that encompassed everyone in the room. The words spoken were spellbinding as we all gazed at the candles of light on the tables. Quietly we geared up for the sleigh ride.

My Christmas Story

My husband really outdid himself. The sleigh was loaded with hay bales for sitting on, apples and corn for the deer. We laughed and locked arms as the sleigh bounced over the rough terrain. Riding on the sleigh through the trees and staring up at the stars and northern lights was an awesome experience. When we reached the back 40 acres of our property, he had prepared a bonfire pit alongside the beaver pond. Within moments, the bales had been unloaded and the fire was roaring. We cuddled up on the bales and sang every Christmas song we knew, and then my father respectfully read the Christmas story from the Bible.

Just when we thought the evening was coming to an end, our son-in-law produced a wonderful array of fireworks, which when rocketing into the sky filled the heavens with color and light. I'm not sure how long we were in the woods. But I know I didn't want it to end. Watching our breath rise like steam in the air as the boom-boom of the fireworks surrounded us was a joyous interlude from the work-a-day lives we lead. All of us were looking up to the heavens on this very special night. All of us were amazed at the festival of lights we had experienced. Those lights were both internal and external. When the fireworks were over, all of us went out onto the beaver pond and made snow angels. Each one left an apple for the deer in their human imprint in the snow. The entire night was a gift filled with laughter and love and gratitude for each other.

I was surprised that our guests didn't leave the house until close to two in the morning. We had celebrated the festival of lights in a sacred way. Everyone left with hearts overflowing with peace knowing they were valued and loved. Isn't that the real meaning of Christmas? We all are valued and loved by a Heavenly Father who gave to us the light of the world on the very first Christmas day.

The Big Storm

Every year at about this time, my husband and I recant the great blizzards we have weathered here on the farm. We tease each other about the endless hours of shoveling to the barn, the manure pile, and back to the house. We laugh about the Halloween storm that left us stranded here at home for three days in 1991. But the worst storm we ever encountered came unexpectedly in late February.

Our girls had just gotten off the bus from school when the snow started. The snowflakes were huge and stunningly beautiful as they fell gently from the sky. The weatherman had predicted four to six inches of snow, which really was average for a storm during late February. My husband was working in Duluth this particular year, and when he got up at 4:30 in the morning, he awakened me. Over eight inches had already fallen, and the wind was picking up. He was on his way to meet his ride share buddies in Barnum and encouraged me to get up and check the school closing reports after going to the barn.

I got up and had a cup of coffee and bundled up for the barn. There was a lot more than eight inches of snow on the deck, so I shoveled my way to the barn, did chores, and was surprised how the wind had drifted in my trail, but undaunted I shoveled my way back to the house. Within an hour the wind had picked up more speed, and at daylight the snow was blowing sideways through the air. Sure enough, school was closed, so I let the girls sleep. I did some laundry, stirred up a batch of cookies and drank all of the coffee. But I had a nagging feeling something was wrong with my husband.

It seems that when he met his buddies at the Little Store, they all jumped into a little Subaru for the trip to Duluth. The freeway was unplowed, and the boys drove where they thought the road was. From what I understand, they were in the median and the ditch more than on the road. After two hours, they had reached work and were five minutes late. All four of them were docked a half hour of pay. None of the other 50 employees made it to work, and as the wind continued to howl and the snow got deeper and deeper, their boss sent them home at 11 a.m. and told them he was paying them for a full day's work.

I got a call from the Little Store in Barnum at one in the afternoon. My husband was going to attempt to drive the pickup to Moose Lake to get some groceries before trying to get home. I gave him a short list and told him to be safe. By four in the afternoon, we had somewhere around 15 inches of snow. But the wind had driven it into huge drifts across the yard and the road. Not knowing what to do, I went out and shoveled and did my barn chores. When I came back into the house, I filled six five-gallon pails with water. If the power went out, we would at least have water for the stock in the morning.

What little daylight we had during the day was fading. It was close to five o'clock when I bundled up again and made my way to the road. I was starting to get concerned that something awful had happened to my husband. The snowdrifts were hip deep, and it was impossible to walk more than 20 feet without having to stop to catch your breath. A quarter of a mile away, I could see him trudging through the snow. I waved my arms at him in the howling wind, and he saw me and waved back. Almost an hour later, he made it to the house. He was pulling a yellow plastic sled with the groceries and 50 pounds of calf feed in it. His clothes were all iced up, and he was soaking wet. He'd been trying to walk the last mile home for more than two hours.

When he got into the house, we cheered him. Then he did something wonderful. He reached into the inside pocket of his jacket and pulled out a one-pound bag of M and Ms, tossed them to me and said, "Honey, I've been thinking about you all day." Funny thing, I'd been thinking about him all day, too.

It took us two days to dig out. I shoveled and he plowed with the tractor. When the driveway was cleared, he hooked the yellow sled up behind the tractor and pulled the girls around the circle drive. There was lots of squealing and laughter. Then he hung the sled in the pole barn. It's still here, and it's just a little reminder that even on the worst of days, we still think about each other.

The Quilt

When I was a teenager, I would sew frequently. I actually learned to sew in junior high school in a home economics course. I enjoyed it even though I was never very good at it. I made myself several dresses and then gave up the sewing machine for a saddle and a horse.

After I was married, I went back to the sewing machine because I had two daughters who always could use a sundress or two over the summer months. I did a significant amount of mending and made a few baby blankets, but the idea of sewing a quilt top made my anxiety soar because I could never sew a straight line.

Fast forward 30 years. I've dug out an old sewing machine, and I'm sewing fleece mittens. The best part about the mittens is that there is a lot of margin for error that goes unnoticed. Somehow I had started to enjoy sewing again. Then I got this wild idea that I should really try a pieced quilt top. How difficult could it really be? When I was at the fabric store searching for just the right mix of patterns and colors, I had a meltdown. It turns out I'm not so good with colors either. But I purchased yards of fabric under the guidance of a friend, which were stunning and earthy.

Sewing was slow. I still was struggling with sewing a straight line. But I worked hard assembling and disassembling and resewing when necessary. I really wanted it to be right. While the machine was slowly joining the small pieces of fabric together, my thoughts in the quiet of the moment were about family and friends. Prayers for health, healing, peace and comfort were all being uttered in time with the slow needle moving up and down on the sewing machine.

Finally after three years and the complication of a broken wrist, the top of the quilt was done. I took it to a quilt shop to have it finished and machine quilted. I was so anxious about having an expert see the quilt top that I was nervous when I showed her my work. She smiled

The Quilt

at me and told me she thought it was beautiful. Three weeks later, she called and told me my lovely quilt was done. I immediately told her it wasn't perfect, but she interrupted me and told me it was one of the most perfect she had ever seen. I was stunned. My response was…"How did that happen?"

So this year I started another winter quilt-top project. The pieces are smaller, and the quilt blocks are more time consuming. Still in the quiet of the house while I am sewing, I find myself praying for family and friends to the slow hum of the sewing machine. I've tried to listen to music or sew to the background noise of the television, but I prefer the quiet time of reflection and prayer when I sew. I didn't understand why I prefer the quiet until recently.

This past winter has been very difficult physically for a kind man from my parish. He has endured open-heart surgery and an unending list of complications. Frankly, he's very blessed to be alive and home again. While I've been sewing over the past months, I've been praying for him. My grandchildren think the world of him. Amazingly enough, he told his wife just a few weeks ago that he has felt like he's been wrapped up in a "quilt" of prayer. He's so grateful to all of his family and friends who have supported him through this difficult time in his life. Why he chose the word *quilt* is a mystery to many but not to me. And maybe that's also why I can now sew a straight line.

Walking the Rim

⋙⋘

For many years, I've had a "bucket list." I'm sure you know exactly what I'm referring to. It's a list of things and places I hope to visit and experience before my aging body can no longer afford me the opportunity. My list is focused from "sea to shining sea" in the United States and revolves around natural wonders. Finally, after years of talking about it, my husband and I made a trip to Arizona in June to visit the Grand Canyon.

I was so excited about the journey that I completed a plethora of research before we even packed our bags. I had formulated an image of what it would be like to stand at the rim and view the Canyon. I had viewed photos and read pages of history. I was so ready that I felt over prepared. When we loaded our suitcases into

Under The Pine Boughs

the truck, I was so excited I squirmed in my seat like a small child. I had a feeling that I knew exactly what I was going to see and experience. The truth is, I was wrong.

We had decided to enter the National Park at the south rim and as we drove on the single lane road, we talked and laughed about what we expected to see. Both of us commented on the change of scenery. We had traveled through the desert and then pines started to appear. The closer we got to the park, the more wooded the countryside was, and as we parked our vehicle, I had the impression that the world fell away just beyond the next tree line.

I'm not going to say I ran to the rim, but almost. When I came through the trees and made my way to the railing, the site before me took my breath away. I was totally unprepared for the majestic, awesome, colorful, vast, beautiful Grand Canyon. We walked for hours along the rim. Sometimes there was a railing, sometimes not. I watched Condors rise up from the canyon, rain falling miles away, and the sun striking the bottom of the canyon displaying the colors of the layers of rock. There were elk standing under the trees close to the rim and

Walking The Rim

a variety of wildlife on the rim trail. Finally, I crawled out to a rock on the edge of the rim and sat down.

I thought about how inadequate my perception of the canyon had been. How my preparation never really prepared me for the actual experience. The grandeur left me speechless. I cried. And then I lifted my hands in praise as a gentle wind blew up from the canyon and tousled my hair. I sat for a long time alone on that rock just soaking up the vista. All too soon, it was time to head back to the car. My husband helped me get back to the rim trail and gave me a kiss and simply said, "awesome."

We rode in silence for a long time, watching for elk and descending back down to the desert. We stopped for ice cream and returned to our hotel. Stunned—we were stunned into silence.

After we returned home, several friends shared with me that the Grand Canyon is also on their bucket list. Because I still am inadequate at explaining the experience, I just simply say…you should go if you can. You'll remember it deep down in your heart, and it will change your perception forever.

CPSIA information can be obtained
at www.ICGtesting.com
Printed in the USA
JSHW021823100919
1425JS00001B/1